THE SEVENTH-DAY ADVENTIST REFORM MOVEMENT

(German Reform)

Helmut H. Kramer

Biblical Research Institute
General Conference of
Seventh-day Adventists

Acknowledgements

Texts credited to NIV are from The New International Version. Copyright © 1978 by New York International Bible Society. Used by permission of Zondervan Publishing House.

Editor's Note

The author of this booklet grew up in a family devoted to the teachings of the Seventh-day Adventist Reform Movement. His father served in its ministry in the United States. Pastor Kramer himself eventually entered the worker force of the Reform Movement and, together with his wife, gave many years of dedicated ministerial service both in the field and later in responsible administrative posts.

In these pages pastor Kramer recounts his pilgrimage of faith which eventually led him and his family to leave the church of his childhood and active labors to become a Seventh-day Adventist. In telling his experience he examines in a kind and honest manner the basic doctrines which separate the Reform Movement from the Seventh-day Adventist Church.

If, after reading this booklet, you hear the call of the Lord to change the direction you have taken in the past—if even to just say, Lord, I want to study these matters further—Pastor Kramer would like to hear from you. You may contact him by writing to him in care of the Biblical Research Institute, General Conference of Seventh-day Adventists, 12501 Old Columbia Pike, Silver Spring, MD 20904

Second printing 1990. Third printing 2000.

Printed in the U.S.A. by the
Review and Herald Publishing Association
Hagerstown, Maryland 21740

Library of Congress Catalog Card Number: 88-152657

ISBN: 0-925675-08-3

Contents

To the Reader

Imagine the following scenario: One Sabbath in church you see a visitor, who by all outward appearances is a conservative Adventist, seemingly well versed in the Scriptures and the Spirit of Prophecy.

To be hospitable, you invite him to your home for lunch. As you converse together, it becomes evident that this visitor is not a member of the Adventist Church. He belongs to another organization which he describes as a movement that upholds the original standards of the Seventh-day Adventist Church.

He informs you that this movement began when the Adventist Church overthrew the commandments of God and told its members to become combatants in warfare at the beginning of World War I. He voices his conviction that the Adventist Church ceased to be the church of God as a result of this transgression. He may even produce documents which seem to indicate that the leaders of the General Conference approved of this improper action, and he will say that the whole church became guilty of the transgression of God's commandments.

These matters take you by surprise. Naturally you ask why you have never heard about these things before. Your visitor tells you that, understandably, the administration of the church tries to keep this as quiet as possible. They do not want the membership to hear about what has taken place.

Your visitor appeals to your sense of fair play. He encourages you to study his group's teachings and to take your stand for God's persecuted few in opposition to those leaders who support open transgression of God's law. He makes it appear that the true Adventist believers in Europe during World War I were disfellowshipped from the church for their faithfulness to the Lord and were persecuted for this.

He will describe the organization of which he is a member as an international movement which upholds the Advent movement in its original objectives and calls people "back to the old paths." He may also express to you the idea that his group did not organize itself until every possible avenue for reunion with the Adventist Church had been tried.

Then your visitor points to statements in the Spirit of Prophecy which tell of a prophesied reformation. He indicates that these prophecies look forward to the establishment of another movement and that the "Reform Movement," of which he is a part, is that movement. He states that in order to be a true child of God you must leave the apostate Seventh-day Adventist Church and become a part of the true remnant people of God—the Seventh-day Adventist Reform Movement—"God's faithful few."

Who are these people who call themselves members of the Seventh-day Adventist Reform Movement? What is the origin of this organization, and what is its history? Are they what they claim to be, or are they impostors? Could it be that they are a people who are honestly deceived into thinking that they are doing the will of God when actually they do not know all the facts?

This booklet will attempt to answer the above questions. The author was reared from birth as a member of the Reform Movement. He served 20 years in the organization as a literature evangelist, pastor, and administrator. Only when he began to see discrepancies between what the organization professed and how it performed, did he start to reexamine some of its teachings and practices.

After attempting to change the direction in which he saw the movement going, he came to the conclusion that its fundamental claims were faulty. Its fundamental right for existence would not bear the test of investigation. Some of its teachings were based upon human reasoning rather than a "thus saith the Lord." As a result of this investigation, he left the Reform Movement and united with the Seventh-day Adventist Church where he now serves as a pastor.

The purpose of this booklet is to reveal in a kindly manner the fallacies of some teachings and attitudes of the Reform Movement. We will point out important misconceptions. Most of the believers in the Reform are dear people who love the Lord and desire nothing more than to do what is right. Many would not remain in the organization if they would study the facts with an open mind, removing all preconceived human reasoning.

The average member of the Reform Movement does not understand the inner workings of the leadership of his organization. He sees, as it were, only a picture that has been glossed over. Members have been so poisoned against the Adventist Church they would rather not attend any church than go to an Adventist service. This is very sad. If they would attend meetings and associate with some faithful Adventist believers, they would realize that they have received many misconceptions about what Adventists believe and how they live. Unfortunately, when they do visit, it is only to contact Adventists with their message or to criticize them.

Reformers then, as this book will show, are a people who need enlightening as to their true condition. They need to be drawn by a loving Christian example to union with God's true Advent movement.

Chapter 1

Who Are These Reformers?

What kind of people make up the Seventh-day Adventist Reform Movement? While we can only generalize, there are certain things which seemingly serve as a common denominator to draw such a group into fellowship. Certain concepts actuate these people, as well as other similar fringe movements, to stand separate from the Adventist Church. We may identify three general classes who gravitate to the movement.

Lifelong Reformers

A large percentage of the membership is composed of people who have been born and raised in the organization. The children are indoctrinated from babyhood in the history of the movement by their parents and church leaders. As a result, lifelong Reformers tend to accept only that information which confirms their earlier training. Since in their minds the Adventist Church is a "fallen church," everything which comes from that source is suspect.

Reformers believe that the writings of Ellen White which were printed since her death have been tampered with by the Adventist leadership. For this reason statements published posthumously which would disprove any teaching which they hold dear are rejected. For example, since Reformers believe that military service in any form is sinful, they discard those statements which give another view, such as the one found in *Selected Messages* regarding military duty in Switzerland (book 2, p. 335).

Even when discussing the early stand of the Adventist pioneers regarding military service, they accept those statements which agree with their position and reject others which do not. In essence, they attempt to rewrite Adventist history. History is reconstructed according to how they believe it must have taken place, rather than according to what the records indicate really happened. Because the members of the Reform Movement are not encouraged to read any material other than what is provided for them, their thinking has, to a great degree, become "inbred." These people are to be deeply pitied because of their ignorance brought about by preconceived opinions.

A great deal of love is shown for their own members. Should a member think of leaving the fellowship, however, he or she is immediately looked upon as an apostate from the truth. The member is no longer worthy of the fellowship of the "saints" and is cut off from all friendship.

It can become very lonely for one who leaves the Reform Movement. Our family experienced such an attitude when we withdrew from the fellowship. This attitude may be responsible for some who stay in the movement despite the evidence of their being deceived. Some pastors tend to remain after they realize the fallacies of the organization because they are not willing to admit that they were deceived. Others fear they will lose their pension. The working policy states this clearly:

> As a decision of the American Union Committee, a minister who remains in good standing, after having completed ten years of service, shall receive 40% of his wages at the time of his termination of service as a pension in case of retirement or disability. *This pension will only be paid to those who have been loyal and faithful to truth and organization and remain so after retirement.* In case of question, the American Union Committee makes the final decision.[1]

Disgruntled Adventists

Another segment of the membership comes from those who have become disgruntled in the Adventist Church for some reason. They may see something with which they do not agree, or feel that they have been neglected, or they share the mentality of those in the Reform Movement that the Adventist Church should take a firmer position on some life-style matters. In reality, the Reform Movement is more a matter of mentality than of doctrine.

For example, there is a general feeling that church leadership should lay down rules of action for every circumstance of life. Once a decision is made, the membership is to conform to it, despite a lack of biblical or Spirit of Prophecy support. The leadership in general is ready to lay down rules for the people. We may cite rulings such as, It is a sin to shave on Sabbath, or, It is a sin to own a television. (This latter issue is not fully complied with by the membership.)

Some local leaders go to great extremes in these matters. In Puerto Rico, for example, I found that the local leader had refused to baptize a person because his family owned a radio. This happened despite the fact

1 *Working Policy of the International Missionary Society of Seventh-day Adventists, Reform Movement, American Union Conference,* p. 11 (emphasis added).

that the General Conference of the movement has not taken such a position. All too frequently area leaders become small dictators over the people.

Reformers tend to adopt the Roman Catholic concept of the authority of the church. While rejecting the decisions of the General Conference of the Seventh-day Adventist Church, they accept the decisions of their own General Conference to the furthest extreme. They take the following statement from the Spirit of Prophecy as giving their General Conference unlimited authority:

> At times, when a small group of men entrusted with the general management of the work have, in the name of the General Conference, sought to carry out unwise plans to restrict God's work, I have said that I could no longer regard the voice of the General Conference, represented by these few men, as the voice of God. But this is not saying that the decisions of a General Conference composed of an assembly of duly appointed, representative men from all parts of the field should not be respected. God has ordained that the representatives of His church from all parts of the earth, when assembled in a General Conference, shall have authority. The error that some are in danger of committing is in giving to the mind and judgment of one man, or of a small group of men, the full measure of authority and influence that God has vested in His church in the judgment and voice of the General Conference assembled to plan for the prosperity and advancement of His work.[2]

This statement has been misused by the Reform leadership due to a poor translation from English into German at the point where the expression "General Conference assembled" reads only "General Conference."[3] The meaning of this statement is then extended to teach that the General Conference is to be regarded as the voice of God to the people with unlimited authority. While the statement taken in context indicates that the General Conference *in session* has authority in deciding how the work is to be advanced, other statements make it clear that this authority in doctrinal matters has certain limits, for example:

> In the commission to His disciples, Christ not only outlined their work, but gave them their message. Teach the people, He

2 Ellen G. White, *Testimonies for the Church* 9 (Mountain View, CA: Pacific Press Publishing Assn., 1948): 260-61.

3 *Schatzkammer, Band 3,* Seite 353-54.

> said, "to observe all things whatsoever I have commanded you." The disciples were to teach what Christ had taught. That which He had spoken, not only in person, but through all the prophets and teachers of the Old Testament, is here included. Human teaching is shut out. There is no place for tradition, for man's theories and conclusions, or for church legislation. No laws ordained by ecclesiastical authority are included in the commission. None of these are Christ's servants to teach. "The law and the prophets," with the record of His own words and deeds, are the treasure committed to the disciples to be given to the world. Christ's name is their watchword, their badge of distinction, their bond of union, the authority for their course of action, and the source of their success. *Nothing that does not bear His superscription is be to recognized in His kingdom.*[4]

This concept is further amplified in the following statement:

> But let us remember that Christian unity does not mean that the identity of one person is to be submerged in that of another; nor does it mean that the mind of one is to be led and controlled by the mind of another. God has not given to any man the power that some, by word and act, seek to claim. God requires every man to stand free and to follow the directions of the word.[5]

New Members

The third general group who make up the ranks of the Reform Movement come directly from other churches or the world. These people are ignorant of the true history of the Advent movement and so can be indoctrinated into the Reform's view of that history. This class forms a large portion of the new converts.

For years, while serving as a pastor and administrator of the movement, I wondered why it was so difficult to obtain converts from the Adventist Church here in America. The reason is now clear to me. American Adventists have full access to the writings of the Spirit of Prophecy as well as the history of their church. Consequently they are not as likely to believe the distorted picture presented by the Reformers.

In most cases it is easier for Reformers to win people from "the world" who do not have an Adventist background. This may not be as true in

4 Ellen G. White, *The Desire of Ages* (Mountain View, CA: Pacific Press Publishing Assn., 1898), p. 826 (emphasis added).

5 *Testimonies for the Church,* 8:212.

countries where the people come from a Catholic background and are more comfortable with authoritarianism. Some of these people may be a bit uncomfortable with the freedom of conscience and the stress on personal responsibility which leads to true Christian growth as found in the Adventist Church.

As stated earlier, Reformers in general are ignorant of the true history of the Advent movement. They have invented their own concept of that history in order to support preconceived ideas of how that history should have taken place. They then search for evidence to confirm these opinions. Many are honestly deceived, but nonetheless deceived.

Spirit of Criticism

A common characteristic found among all classes of Reformers is the disposition to criticize everyone, especially the Adventist Church. Such an attitude permeates the movement and even affects some of its teachings. Often the thought is expressed, Let us not accept this doctrine since that would make us too much like the Adventist Church. For many years the writer of this booklet suscribed to the *Adventist Review* in order to find something that could be used to prove the Adventist Church had fallen further into apostasy. The following statement from the pen of inspiration applies forcefully to this critical spirit:

> Satan is "the accuser of the brethren," and it is his spirit that inspires men to watch for the errors and defects of the Lord's people, and to hold them up to notice, while their good deeds are passed by without a mention.[6]

How much better it would be if Reformers would take as their motto the instruction found in Philippians 4:8—

> Finally, brethren, whatsoever things are true, whatsoever things are honest, whatsoever things are just, whatsoever things are pure, whatsoever things are lovely, whatsoever things are of good report; if there be any virtue, and if there be any praise, think on these things.

6 Ellen G. White, *The Great Controversy* (Mountain View, CA: Pacific Press Publishing Assn., 1950), p. 395.

Chapter 2

Origin of the Seventh-day Adventist Reform Movement

In many parts of the world field today Adventists are confronted by a hostile organization calling itself the Seventh-day Adventist Reform Movement. Sometimes this group is designated as the "German Reform Movement" because it originated in Germany. In actuality there are presently two major organizations since a split occurred in 1951. Since this separation much time has been spent by the opposing factions in fighting each other and in dealing with dissension in the ranks. As a result they have had less time and energy for fighting the Adventist Church.

Both organizations carry almost identical names. However, one faction also refers to itself as the International Missionary Society. Their common origin stems from the mistakes made by certain Adventist Church leaders in Europe at the beginning of World War I. For ease of identification I will use the initials IMS for the International Missionary Society faction and '51 Movement for the faction which separated from the IMS during a power struggle in 1951.

German Adventism Before and During World War I

In order to understand the origin of the Reform Movement during World War I in its proper context, it is necessary to understand a little about the Adventist work in Europe in contrast with that in America. It is also necessary to understand the direction taken by the European church leadership as the opening of World War I approached. And it is helpful to compare the mentality of the European with that of the American in order to comprehend how this movement could come into being.

Elder L. R. Conradi (1856-1939), a German migrant to America, accepted the Seventh-day Adventist message in Iowa (1878). Eight years later (1886) the denomination sent him to work in Europe where he fostered a rapid advance of the church in Germany. He became the main pillar in German Adventism, as well as in other areas of Europe. His strong leadership continued for about 35 years. Under his administration the work seemed to prosper. Even Ellen White testified in 1901 that Conradi "[had] been doing the work of several men."[1]

While on the surface all seemed to be going well, there were subtle influences at work which would later affect the church in Europe negatively for many years. It seems likely that some German nationalism began to creep into Conradi's work. He began to downgrade the Millerite movement in America as well as the importance of the Spirit of Prophecy.

> While translating and revising J. N. Andrew's *History of the Sabbath,* Conradi delved deeply into the writings of the Protestant reformers. He became more and more attracted to the idea that it was actually Luther who had heralded the three angels' messages. This led him to downgrade the entire Millerite movement in America. It seems possible that his views were taking on some of the German nationalistic coloration so prevalent in his area of labor during the pre-World War I period. Some believed that his disenchantment with Ellen White was due to the fact that she did not fit the role of the good German "housfrau," content to play a subordinate role in church affairs.[2]

Meanwhile difficulties were being encountered in Europe, which did not exist in America, especially in the realm of Sabbath observance and military service. Children were required by law to attend school on Sabbath. The best exception church leaders were able to arrange with the government allowed the children to study their Bibles in school on Sabbath, but they had to be in attendance.[3] Records indicate that Adventist young people complied with the required military duty during peace time, but they frequently went to prison for their refusal to work and fulfill duty on the Sabbath.[4]

While in Europe even Ellen White, as we alluded to earlier, had to face the situation of a peacetime military draft of the brethren in Switzerland. This might come as a surprise to some, but she did not speak out against the brethren being in the military but rather encouraged them to be faithful. This matter will be covered in greater detail in a later chapter.

Ellen White was in full agreement with the teaching of John the Baptist when he was questioned by the Roman soldiers. They asked him for

---

1 R. W. Schwarz, *Light Bearers to the Remnant* (Mountain View, CA: Pacific Press Publishing Association, 1979), p. 475.

2 Ibid.

3 Ibid., p. 220.

4 Ibid., p. 219; also, O. Kramer Experiences (my father).

information regarding their duty. "Then some soldiers asked him, 'And what should we do?' He replied, 'Don't extort money and don't accuse people falsely—be content with your pay' " (Luke 3:14-15, NIV). Notice that he did not tell them that they must resign from the military.

At the beginning of World War I, when additional pressure was placed on our leaders by the government, some buckled and instructed the church members to serve in the military on the Sabbath as other warriors do on Sunday. In a letter addressed to the Ministry of War in Berlin on August 4, 1914, the following declaration was made:

> Most Honorable Lord General and Minister of War:
>
> Since ofttimes our point of view concerning our duty towards the Government, also our position in general military duty; and especially, since our refusal to serve, in times of peace, on Saturday (Sabbath) is regarded as fanatical, therefore I take the liberty, Your Excellency, to present to you in the following, the principles of German Seventh-day Adventists, especially just now, in the present war situation.
>
> While we stand on the fundamentals of the Holy Scriptures, and seek to fulfill the precepts of Christendom, keeping the Rest Day (Saturday) that God established in the beginning, by endeavoring to put aside all work on that day, still in these times of stress, we have bound ourselves together in defense of the "Fatherland," and under these circumstances we will also bear arms on Saturday (Sabbath). On this point we take our stand on the Scripture found in 1 Peter 2:13-17. (Signed) H. F. Schuberth, President.

The next March (1915) several of the Division leaders, including L. R. Conradi, signed an additional letter which affirmed their agreement with this position. While this later statement was sent in the name of the European Division, it did not have the support of every member of the Division Committee. Some of these members were strongly opposed to what they considered to be an improper position.

Development of Protest

This position on combatant service, as well as duty on the Sabbath, stood clearly in opposition to the traditional position taken by Adventists during the United States Civil War. When our German members were confronted with this new position, many began to protest, just as many protested a similar suggestion made by James White during the Civil War in America. Instead of praying quietly about the matter and seeking for wisdom from the Lord, they followed in the footsteps of some believers in Civil War times. Ellen White described the situation then:

> In Iowa they carried things to quite a length, and ran into fanaticism. They mistook zeal and fanaticism for conscientiousness. Instead of being guided by reason and sound judgment, they allowed their feelings to take the lead. They were ready to become martyrs for their faith. Did all this feeling lead them to God? to greater humility before Him? Did it lead them to trust in His power to deliver them from the trying position into which they might be brought? Oh, no! Instead of making their petitions to the God of heaven and relying solely upon His power, they petitioned the legislature and were refused. They showed their weakness and exposed their lack of faith. All this only served to bring that peculiar class, Sabbathkeepers, into special notice, and expose them to be crowded into difficult places by those who have no sympathy for them.[5]

So it was that some members who opposed this new and improper position taken by a few leaders in Europe at the beginning of World War I began to protest vigorously. This protest seems to have been especially strong in Bremen, Germany. The opposition in this city became very vocal against the church's leadership. The protests were so strong that conference leadership had to be called to quell the discontent which had been generated. Meetings of the church had been disrupted by these protests. They could not even be completed with song and prayer.[6]

These protesters, no doubt, meant well; nonetheless their dissension disrupted the worship services in the church. As was the case during the American Civil War, these protesting members "mistook zeal and fanaticism for conscientiousness." This situation caused the leadership to react with further improper actions and they disfellowshipped the protesters without due process. This in turn caused more hard feelings and alienation to build up, along with a spirit of antagonism and persecution on both sides of the issue. How much better it would have been if all the believers had heeded the injunction of the Spirit of Prophecy given to the American Adventists during the Civil War:

> Those who would be best prepared to sacrifice even life, if required, rather than place themselves in a position where they could not obey God, would have the least to say. They would

5 *Testimonies for the Church,* 1:356-57.

6 This testimony is from O. Kramer, my father, who was there as a young person.

> make no boast. They would feel deeply and meditate much, and their earnest prayers would go up to heaven for wisdom to act and grace to endure. Those who feel that in the fear of God they cannot conscientiously engage in this war will be very quiet, and when interrogated will simply state what they are obliged to say in order to answer the inquirer, and then let it be understood that they have no sympathy with the Rebellion.[7]

The disfellowshipped members then began an open war against the Adventist Church, a "war" which became very bitter at times. Those who opposed participation in military warfare now turned their weapons against the church and sought to discredit its leadership and people.

Since the disfellowshipped ones were not organized at this time, various outspoken individuals would arise, claiming to be part of the group. It soon became difficult to know who was or was not associated with the dissenters. As a result of the fanatical actions of some who claimed to be Reformers, the leadership of the Adventist Church was further alienated and concluded that the entire movement was composed of such people. This, of course, weakened the possibilities for reunion later.

Certain persons claimed to have been given visions about the timing for the close of probation. The Reformers of today, however, totally discount and deny that these persons were a part of their movement. Whether they were is not really the question. The point is that they were perceived by church leadership to be a part of the movement.

Very foolish and evil actions were committed by some of these dissidents who printed controversial tracts and gave the impression that they were published by the Adventist publishing house. Others went so far as to demand that the church properties be turned over to them.

The man who later became the main spokesman for the movement, Edmond Doerschler, made the claim that the church officials had stolen the church properties from the true believers. It is of interest to note that he was the very person who was chosen to represent the disfellowshipped members before the brethren of the General Conference in 1920.[8] Because he was the group's spokesman, his words were taken by the church's leadership as representing the feelings of the entire movement.

In 1919, before the disfellowshipped members had determined officially what stand the Adventist General Conference had taken in this matter of military service, they published 10,000 copies of a pamphlet describing the Adventist Church as the great apostate woman. This pamphlet had

---

7 *Testimonies for the Church,* 1:357.
8 *Report of a Meeting With the Opposition Movement,* July 21-23, 1920, in Friedensau, p. 21.

pictures of the true church of Revelation 12 and the apostate church of Revelation 17. In the document they attempted to prove from the writings of Ellen White that the words "Babylon is fallen" applied to Seventh-day Adventists.[9] This was done despite the fact that she expressly stated that no such accusation was ever to be made.

> When anyone arises, either among us or outside of us, who is burdened with a message which declares that the people of God are numbered with Babylon, and claims that the loud cry is a call to come out of her, you may know that he is not bearing the message of truth. Receive him not, nor bid him Godspeed; for God has not spoken by him, neither has He given a message to him, but he has run before he was sent.[10]

Apparently the early Reformers were ignorant of this statement. Since being confronted with this and similar statements from the pen of inspiration, they have been more careful in recent years with their terminology. The bottom line of their message, however, is still the same: "The church is fallen, and we are now the true Adventists. Your salvation depends on your being a part of the 'Faithful Few.' " They even go so far as to rationalize the above statement by stressing the words, "he has run before he was sent." To them this phrase means that the time would come when such a declaration would be given. Such a conclusion is drawn despite the clear underlying message to the contrary.

In 1919 the disfellowshipped members organized themselves into a church body under the name (loosely translated) "International Missionary Society of Seventh-day Adventists, old since 1844 firm-standing direction, German Union standing since 1844." The title, in itself, revealed the dissidents' ignorance of Adventist history. Later, when statements in the Spirit of Prophecy were found which spoke of a reformatory movement, they saw themselves as a fulfillment of such a prophecy. For this reason the new organization changed its name to the Seventh-day Adventist Reform Movement.

Attempts to Resolve the German Situation

When the Adventist General Conference president, Elder A. G. Daniells, arrived in Germany in 1920 to examine the matters of conflict, he did not meet with a dissident group of believers who had remained

9 Ibid., p. 23.
10 Ellen G. White, *Testimonies to Ministers* (Mountain View, CA: Pacific Press Publishing Association, 1962), p. 41.

faithful to the church and its doctrines. By this time he was obliged to face a full-fledged organization which had already begun to work in opposition to the church and its leadership. In addition, the movement had been taken over by certain unstable and unreasonable men.

Both spokesmen for the disfellowshipped group at the 1920 meeting later left the Reform Movement. Edmond Doerschler, the main speaker, established his own movement in Holland one year later. There he acted as a prince over his members in a very un-Christian manner and eventually died in an institution for the mentally ill. The other spokesman, H. Spanknobel, later became a Nazi.

The discussions held with Elder Daniells revealed that the leaders of the Reform group had been committing many of the errors they had accused their Adventist leaders of committing. This was especially true in regard to arbitrary actions against members who did not agree with the leaders. There were several instances where Reformers had been disfellowshipped from their own movement without due process, by a committee rather than by the church according to proper church order. It seemed as if the Reformers were too proud, however, to admit that they could have done anything wrong.

This position is still the watchword today. Reform leadership still refuses to admit that it can make mistakes. The General Conference president of the IMS faction of the movement takes a position just one step short of being infallible. To disagree with any of his decisions simply prepares the way for dismissal from the church, especially if you are a worker. Please note some recent pronouncements in this regard:

In the charter of the Reform Movement's General Conference (IMS) which was redone and registered in 1973, is the following statement:

> If a member of the Board, mentioned in P. 5 (Board of trustees), or a delegate of the society, violates the Bible principles, or is against the written and *unwritten* order of our denomination, the person at fault may, by a simple plurality of votes of the meeting of the society, be taken out of office and be excommunicated from the church.[11]

As I learned from first-hand experience, the unwritten order was to obey unquestionably every wish of the General Conference president.

At the 1983 General Conference Session (IMS) a series of conditions were laid down by the Reform General Conference president which included: "Every member of the G.C. Committee commits himself to live

11 Charter of the International Missionary Society of the Seventh-day Adventists, Reform Movement, General Conference—1973 (emphases added).

faithfully to the Principles, to carry out the instructions of the president, and not to institute a rebellion."[12] Previously when the president was asked by a member of the General Conference Committee why he had acted directly contrary to the decisions made by the Committee, his answer was that the Committee was only advisory.

The Reformers in Germany held to European concepts of authoritarianism. They could not understand the approach of working in a loving manner with an erring member rather than immediately disfellowshipping him if he did not follow unquestioningly the decisions of church leadership. They became offended by the fact that the Adventist General Conference, after declaring that members should be noncombatants, did not condemn and disfellowship those who did not see matters in the same light during World War I.

Since the Adventist General Conference did not immediately disband the division and disfellowship the leaders as punishment for their sins, Reformers assert that the General Conference became responsible and in reality approved their mistakes. In this they are ignorant of simple order and organization. This is clearly pointed out by Elder L. H. Christian:

> A Division of the General Conference was at that time a regularly incorporated body with a constitution and a constituency. Such a Division can only be organized or disbanded at a quadrennial session of the General Conference. The first such session of the General Conference after the beginning of the First World War, convened in San Francisco in 1918.[13]

The European Division was terminated later that year. The General Conference leadership in the Reform Movement believes that it has the right to replace a union president if he makes what the General Conference leadership considers to be a mistake, without even consulting the constituency. Not only do they believe in this practice, they have frequently exercised this supposed authority. They neglect the instruction of the Spirit of Prophecy which states, "The fact that men make mistakes is no reason why we should think them unfit to be caretakers."[14] God would reclaim.

When Elder Daniells and several other brethren from the Adventist General Conference in America met with the spokesmen of the Reform group, the latter posed four questions to them. The Reformers later claimed that because they received no satisfactory answers to their questions no reunion could take place.

---

12 *The Sabbath Watchman*, January/February 1984.
13 L. H. Christian, *The Aftermath of Fanaticism or a Counterfeit Reformation*, p. 21.
14 *Testimonies to Ministers*, p. 304.

By presenting only half the story, the Reformers make it appear that the failure to reunite lay with Elder Daniells. The truth is that they were greatly at fault themselves. Elder Daniells and his coworkers asked the Reformers many important questions of which, sad to say, most Reformers are not aware. I personally did not know about these questions, despite the fact that I was born and reared in the Reform Movement. It was not until after I left the movement that I researched these matters for myself.

These questions were an embarrassment to the Reform spokesmen. The questions posed by the Adventist leadership included those asking for the rationale for some of the terrible accusations made by the Reformers against the church. One question voiced by Elder Daniells was, "Is it your idea that this picture of the true church represents your organization and that this other picture of the apostate church represents our organization?" To this question the Reform spokesmen, after admitting that they did not know what stand the American brethren had taken in the recent war, answered, "Here in Germany . . . we represent the right church and they represent the apostate."[15]

The Reformers took the stance that even doing medical work in the military was "devil service." Elder Daniells could not accept this extreme position in light of the historical stand of Adventists during the Civil War. The record indicates that they were willing to participate in military service as long as they would not have to violate their consciences. This was also the position taken by the American brethren during World War I.

Elder Daniells pointed out that in the recent conflict some brethren in America had difficulty in determining the proper position to take, just as had been the case in the Civil War. After extended discussion, they decided on the same position the church had taken in the Civil War and declared themselves noncombatants. He went on to state, however, that there were honest differences of opinion as to what were the proper limits in fulfilling such a position. The Adventist leader then stated that the final determination of what was right and wrong must be left to the individual conscience of the member.

This latter statement deeply offended the Reformers who felt that the church must take the responsibility for the conscience of each of its members. In Reform thinking there is no place for individual responsibility toward God. To the contrary, corporate responsibility must be exercised on the part of the church for every member. Many want every duty determined by the church leadership. This position fails to take into consideration such statements as the following:

---

15 *Report of a Meeting With the Opposition Movement*, July 21-23, 1920, in Friedensau, p. 32.

> In matters of conscience the soul must be left untrammeled. No one is to control another's mind, to be judge for another, or to prescribe his duty. God gives to every soul freedom to think, and to follow his own convictions. "Every one of us shall give account of himself to God." No one has the right to merge his own individuality in that of another. In all matters where principle is involved, "let every man be fully persuaded in his own mind." Rom. 14:12, 5. In Christ's kingdom there is no lordly oppression, no compulsion of manner. The angels of heaven do not come to the earth to rule, and to exact homage, but as messengers of mercy, to co-operate with man in uplifting humanity.[16]

> As a people our faith and practice need to be energized by the Holy Spirit. No ruling power that would compel man to obey the dictates of the finite mind should be exercised. "Cease ye from man, whose breath is in his nostrils," the Lord commands. By turning the minds of men to lean on human wisdom, we place a veil between God and man, so that there is not a seeing of Him who is invisible.[17]

The leadership of the Reform Movement in general is willing to supply direction for every detail of life for its membership. The General Conference leadership demands that all material prepared for publication in any part of the world must first be approved first by them. In this way a few men at the top control what everyone believes. There is no room for originality of thought or research on the part of members or even workers. The leadership does not trust anyone, not even the properly elected literature committees in different countries. The General Conference leaders do not like to allow these committees to choose what is published. Please note the instruction from the Pen of Inspiration regarding this matter:

> When men in any line of God's work seek to bring the minds and talents of the Lord's human agents under their control, they have assumed a jurisdiction over their fellowmen that they cannot maintain without injustice and iniquity. The Lord has placed no man as judge, either of the pen or the voice of God's workmen.[18]

16 *The Desire of Ages,* pp. 550-51.
17 *Testimonies to Ministers,* p. 483.
18 Ibid., p. 293.

Reform Movement Mind-Set

The mind-set of the Reform Movement has made it impossible to work toward unity between this organization and the Adventist Church. It is this mind-set more than anything else which separates the two organizations. The Adventist Church follows the instruction of the Spirit of Prophecy that for every doctrine we are to demand a plain "Thus saith the Lord." (See *The Great Controversy,* p. 595). The Reform Movement holds the right to legislate for the people in cases where the Word is silent and in other situations as well, even when the Spirit of Prophecy states just the opposite. By assuming this position the organization has returned to the authoritarianism of the Roman Church.

> Rome withheld the Bible from the people and required all men to accept her teachings in its place. It was the work of the Reformation to restore to men the word of God; but is it not too true that in the churches of our time men are taught to rest their faith upon their creed and the teachings of their church rather than on the Scriptures?[19]

It is a sad fact that Reformers place greater confidence in the "Principles of Faith," their fundamental statement of belief, than they do in the Bible. This booklet has become an unbending creed.

Reformers feel strongly that their organization embraces God's special people and that the movement can do no wrong. On one occasion I reported to the president of the General Conference about a cordial visit I had made with a high official of the Adventist Church. He replied, "There are some faithful people in the Adventist Church, and they will eventually join the Reform Movement." So much for the Reformers' spiritual pride.

Since the separation between the Reformers and the Seventh-day Adventist Church in 1914, several attempts at reunion have been made. The first, which has already been mentioned, took place in 1920 when Elder Daniells met with the Reform spokesmen. In 1922 the Reformers requested a hearing at the General Conference Session in San Francisco. This was not granted by Elder Daniells, due to his unfruitful experience in 1920. In retrospect, this probably was a mistake on his part, but the decision is understandable in light of his previous experience. Since that time there have been other meetings. These have likewise ended in failure due to the unbending and self-righteous spirit of the Reform leaders who believe that Adventists must come around to accept the Reform view in order to stand right in the sight of God.

---

19 *The Great Controversy,* p. 388.

Reformers have taken the position that they have been called by God to further their movement and that the Adventist Church has apostatized from the truth. As a result even the Spirit of Prophecy books published since the death of Ellen White are suspect. In this manner they cut themselves off from instruction which could correct their mistaken ideas.

Even if the matter of military service could be resolved in harmony with the Reformers' position of total conscientious objection (refusal to participate in any way with the military), the majority of the Reformers would still reject unification with the Adventist Church. They would find other reasons for being a separate movement. The members are constantly filled with evil reports regarding the actions of Adventists in various parts of the world. They are, without question, crusaders for separation from the Adventist Church.

Through the years, since the separation in 1914, the movement has adopted other teachings which are deviant from Adventist beliefs. Today the leadership holds tenaciously to these doctrines, despite all proof from the Bible and Spirit of Prophecy to the contrary. This matter will be dealt with in another chapter.

Chapter 3

History of the Seventh-day Adventist Reform Movement

As a guideline for verifying spiritual claims, Jesus gave His well-known "orchard test"—"by their fruits ye shall know them" (Matt 7:20). The reader may apply the test for himself as we turn now to trace the later history of the Reform Movement.

We have seen that the Seventh-day Adventist Reform Movement began in what may seem as a well-founded protest against the wrong position taken by some of the leaders of the Adventist Church in Europe at the outbreak of World War I. We have observed also that the movement acted presumptuously in organizing itself into an active force against its mother church before adequate attempts could be made for reunion.

Spiritual pride, manifested by its leaders, prevented reunion in 1920 and at all subsequent attempts. The questions naturally arise, What has been the history of the movement from that momentous time of separation (1914) until the present? Do we see evidence that the Reform has a special calling from God and that it has received His special blessing?

Reformers believe that their movement is a fulfillment of prophecy and that they are called by God to give the last message of warning to the world. They consider the Adventist Church to have apostatized. They assume their movement to be a fulfillment of the prophesied reformation spoken of in the *Testimonies:*

> In visions of the night, representations passed before me of a great reformatory movement among God's people. Many were praising God. The sick were healed, and other miracles were wrought. A spirit of intercession was seen, even as was manifested before the great Day of Pentecost. Hundreds and thousands were seen visiting families and opening before them the word of God. Hearts were convicted by the power of the Holy Spirit, and a spirit of genuine conversion was manifest. On every side doors were thrown open to the proclamation of the

> truth. The world seemed lightened with the heavenly influence. Great blessings were received by the true and humble people of God. I heard voices of thanksgiving and praise, and there seemed to be a reformation such as we witnessed in 1844.[1]

Even the most optimistic Reformers realize that this description in no way represents the true condition of the Reform today, or at any time in its history. They hope that such a condition will come to fruition sometime in the future.

After the ill-fated attempts at reunion with the Adventist Church in 1920 and 1922, the Reformers set out to carry their message to the world. They organized a General Conference in 1925, at which time they set down the movement's fundamental beliefs and organizational rules in a booklet entitled, *The Principles of Faith and Church By-laws.* The writing was done, no doubt in good faith, according to the information available to them. The Reformers had limited access to the *Testimonies* of the Spirit of Prophecy because they lacked adequate knowledge of the English language. Only a small number of Ellen White's writings were available in German. Consequently a number of teachings not in harmony with basic Adventist beliefs or with the Spirit of Prophecy were adopted at this time. This is understandable and forgivable. What is not understandable, however, is what has happened as more Testimonies have become available to them and further light has been revealed. The reason lies in the Reformers' basic motto.

A Motto Misapplied

One of the watchwords of the Reform Movement is "back to the old paths." (See Jeremiah 6:16.) The problem is that they often do not know what the old paths are. As they tried to hold to the "old paths" over the years, they also picked up old errors and held tenaciously to them, regardless of any evidence to the contrary.

Some Reform leaders hold errors taught by early Adventists. One example is the position certain leaders hold regarding the nature of Christ. Since pioneers such as Uriah Smith, at least at one point in his experience, believed Christ was a created being, some Reformers likewise hold to this teaching. To them this is the old path of the Advent pioneers and must be right. In so doing they reject the clear statements from the Spirit of Prophecy regarding this matter.

In the first organizational name they adopted they made the claim that they held to the teachings of the Advent Movement *in 1844.* They still

1 *Testimonies for the Church,* 9:126.

make this claim which shows that they do not have even a correct factual knowledge of the history of the Adventist Church. To hold to the teachings of 1844 would mean that their members should be Sunday keepers, swine eaters, and smokers.

The claim overlooks the fact that truth for the Advent people was and should be progressive. As a result of this misconception, the teachings in the Reform Movement have become petrified, limited to the views of their early leaders with no room for further spiritual unfolding. Workers have been dismissed for teaching that Christ possessed divinity while on earth, despite the fact that the Bible, as well as the Spirit of Prophecy, is extremely clear on this matter. We will touch on this again.

The Reformers' motto of "back to the old paths" prevents correction of the "Principles of Faith." The leaders realize that there are definite mistakes in this booklet, but they do not wish to admit their forefathers could have made any mistakes. Consequently the booklet remains as first adopted without even editorial corrections.

For example, the leadership has even refused to correct typographical errors such as the citation of Bible passages which do not exist. In another case, the booklet incorrectly quotes the Spirit of Prophecy. The "Principles" booklet states:

> Sister White writes concerning this. The volumes of "Spirit of Prophecy," and also the "Testimonies," should be introduced into every Sabbath-keeping family. *Also the books should be offered by the church to everyone at a low figure,* and also be found in the libraries.[2]

When we read the original, an entirely opposite message is given:

> The volumes of *Spirit of Prophecy,* and also the *Testimonies,* should be introduced into every Sabbathkeeping family, and the brethren should know their value and be urged to read them. It is not a wise plan to place these books at a low figure and have only one set in a church. They should be in the library of every family and read again and again. Let them be kept where they can be read by many, and let them be worn out in being read by all the neighbors.[3]

Even the knowledge of such glaring errors does not overcome the Reform leaders' fear of making any changes in this important document.

---

2 *The Principles of Faith of the Seventh-day Adventist Church, "Reform Movement,"* pp. 10-11 (emphasis added).

3 *Testimonies for the Church,* 4:390 (emphasis added).

In 1978, the Reform General Conference (IMS) delegates in session voted unanimously to rewrite this booklet. When such a revision was attempted in the General Conference Committee, it quickly became apparent that such a rewriting would be impossible. Some leaders in high authority seem to believe that to change even a comma would be apostasy from the faith.

As recently as 1983 General Conference Committee members were required to abide by certain conditions. One statement reads, "[He] commits himself to live faithfully to the Principles."[4] In this way the Reformers affirm their creed and refuse to come to grips with the errors found in the document. The following statements by Ellen White fittingly describe their actions:

> Some have feared that if in even a single point they acknowledge themselves in error, other minds would be led to doubt the whole theory of truth. Therefore they have felt that investigation should not be permitted, that it would tend to dissension and disunion. But if such is to be the result of investigation, the sooner it comes the better. If there are those whose faith in God's word will not stand the test of an investigation of the Scriptures, the sooner they are revealed the better; for then the way will be opened to show them their error. We cannot hold that a position once taken, an idea once advocated, is not, under any circumstances, to be relinquished. There is but One who is infallible—He who is the way, the truth, and the life.[5]

> Those who profess to be servants of the living God must be willing to be servants of all, instead of being exalted above the brethren, and they must possess a kind, courteous spirit. If they err, they should be ready to confess thoroughly. Honesty of intention cannot stand as an excuse for not confessing errors. Confession would not lessen the confidence of the church in the messenger, and he would set a good example; a spirit of confession would be encouraged in the church, and sweet union would be the result.[6]

After the organization of the Reform in 1925, different workers were sent into the world field to bring the Reform message to the various continents. One worker went to South America to establish the work there.

---

4 *The Sabbath Watchman,* January/February 1984.

5 *Testimonies to Ministers,* p. 105.

6 Ellen G. White, *Early Writings* (Washington, DC: Review & Herald Publishing Assn., 1945), pp. 102-3.

Several traveled to the United States and eventually organized the American Union. But through the years the American Union has been a trouble spot for the dictatorial leadership of the movement headquartered in Germany.

It seems that even though the workers sent to America were Germans, they soon began to breathe the free air of the United States and would no longer be subject to dictatorship. As they learned the English language and were able to read extensively in the Spirit of Prophecy, they would begin to entertain views differing from their German leaders. Again and again attempts were made to force the American movement into conformity with the General Conference in Germany. I have in my possession documents which reveal a power struggle which lasted for about 40 years until the Americans finally submitted to this uncontrolled dictatorship in 1982.

It is not the purpose of the writer to disclose all the terrible details of the spirit which has worked in the movement from its very beginning until the present day. Such an exposé would not serve to build up anyone spiritually. However, the facts are that over the years there has been a constant battle for the leadership of the movement, with one uprising after another.

As background to a later development, it may be said that one of the blackest spots in Reform history occurred in connection with one of the General Conference presidents. This man published a book and included statements from the Spirit of Prophecy which he altered to fit his supposed higher ideas of sexual morality. Later, the president was found guilty of committing adultery.

We cannot, of course, judge a movement by just one of its leaders. We are all sinners and all are in the need of God's grace and forgiveness. However, there are still some administrators in the movement who hold to this former leader's so-called higher standard of family living, namely, that husbands and wives should live "as brother and sister."

Since the Reform leaders in America opposed this unbiblical position, they were branded as rebels and opposers of church order. This unrighteous branding laid the foundation for the separation which took place in the Reform Movement, beginning in 1948 and culminating in 1951.

The Great Reform Schism

In 1948 the General Conference leadership in Germany decided to act decisively to bring the American Union under its domination and to transfer the movement's headquarters to the United States. A worker, previously known for his high-handed actions in Australia, was assigned to the United States to reorganize the work in the American Union. When the

American leaders refused to hand over the leadership as demanded, this official, with one stroke of the pen, dissolved the entire American Union and disfellowshipped its leaders. This arbitrary action agitated a conflict which caused the majority of the members in America to withdraw from the movement entirely. Some returned to the Seventh-day Adventist Church, while others gave up their faith completely.

In 1951, at another Reform General Conference session, the same official, who had on his own supposed authority dissolved the American Union, staged a rebellion himself in an attempt to become president of the General Conference. When he was not able to get his wishes, he withdrew with about 45 percent of the delegates and organized a new movement. He had already secured, in a devious manner, a hold on much of the property. These bold actions resulted in a court case in which the two groups fought each other for the right to use the name and the properties. The case was settled out of court with the understanding that there was to be no further litigation regarding the name. For this reason there are two "Reform Movements" today, each claiming to be the original one.

As previously stated, in order to facilitate a clear identity of the two major factions which resulted from the "Great Schism" of 1951, I will refer to them as follows: (1) IMS—("International Missionary Society"). This is the original movement of which I was a member. This group has its General Conference headquarters in West Germany. (2) The '51 Movement. This is the group which separated from the IMS in 1951. I understand that their General Conference is now located in Roanoke, Virginia, U.S.A. It is necessary to differentiate between these two groups because they have a common origin and both use the same name, "Seventh-day Adventist Reform Movement," or some variation thereof.

There have been several futile attempts to reunite these two factions of the Reform Movement. The most notable attempt took place in 1967 at a General Conference session of the '51 Reform Movement in Brazil. An appointed "peace committee," after examining all the documents and interviewing the leaders of their faction who were involved in the split of 1951, came to the conclusion that "there is no difference between us in principle[s of faith]."[7] Despite such a conclusion, reunion did not take place. Some leaders feared that they would lose their positions of power; they were also unwilling to admit they had made any mistakes. It is evident, however, that both movements tenaciously hold the same false teachings reviewed in this book.

The separation in 1951 came about as a result of strife over the leadership of the movement. Still today each faction attempts to take members

7 *Peace Committee Report* ('51 Movement), Sao Paulo, Brazil, September 4, 1967.

away from the other. Only their antagonism for each other surpasses their feelings against the Adventist Church. In 1952 the American Union, which had in name been disfellowshipped from the movement, was again united with the General Conference of the "International Missionary Society" faction of the Reform Movement. In later years the struggle for supremacy between the American Union and the General Conference (IMS) came to the foreground once again. In 1982 the president of the General Conference, with high-handed, illegal actions, tried to force the American Union to submit completely to his control.

The movement experienced difficulties not only in the United States but in other areas as well. In 1978 I was elected to serve as president of the North American Division of the Seventh-day Adventist Reform Movement (IMS). This division included all the area from Canada to Panama. I received instruction from the General Conference (IMS) leadership to "clean up the mess" in Central America and Mexico. The conditions I found there still make me shudder to this day.

I discovered leaders holding church properties in their own personal names. There was a total lack of record keeping. One conference president was unfaithful to his wife and had to be asked to resign. Fanaticism was rampant. Each leader imposed his brand of health and dress reform on the membership without any proof from the Bible, Spirit of Prophecy, or scientific evidence.

In Mexico, for example, the very essence of the health message was not to mix salty and sweet foods at meals. The union president taught that this counsel came from the writings of the Spirit of Prophecy which, of course, was not the case. The predominant doctrine taught to the people related to dress. The people adopted the standards held by the local leader. The members were much more concerned with externals than with the condition of the heart and a loving spirit toward their fellowman.

I could also speak about the conference where the delegates found it necessary to remove the previous leaders from office. They revoked their credentials because of misconduct and unchristian attitudes, and because they refused to turn over church properties to the properly elected officers. The newly elected president was a humble servant of the Lord.

A short time later the former leaders staged a revolt and again took over the leadership of the church. When this became known, the General Conference (IMS) leadership chose to do nothing because it was not politically expedient. This happened despite the fact that the General Conference leaders knew all about the corruption of these men. They chose to allow the membership to suffer abuse rather than take action on their behalf.

When this took place, I resigned as division president. I could not accept this ungodly action on the part of those who made such high claims. The Reformers constantly claim to hold high standards, but in regard to organizational matters in the movement, there is total chaos. It is a matter of the survival of the most powerful.

In one conference, as reported by the members, the Lord's Supper had seldom been celebrated. There had been few if any baptisms. But the president had disfellowshipped many members whom he felt were subversive. In most cases the leader had done this without even taking the matter before the church.

In justice to this leader, I would say that his arbitrary actions should not be attributed to willful misconduct. As I see it, his mistakes were due to a lack of education. He had been sent to work in this field with little or no instruction, and no salary. He had done the best he could with the limitations imposed on him. This brings up another important point—the matter of education.

Attitudes Toward Education

Ellen White speaks much about the importance of proper education. As a result, Adventists in general are more highly educated than the general population. The case with the Reform Movement is exactly the opposite. Until recent years they have discouraged their young people from obtaining an education, especially a college education. In one country in Central America, I found that the leader had advised even those in elementary school to quit since, according to him, education could be harmful to their spiritual life. For many years the Reform Movement (IMS) had only a school for missionary workers in Germany. To attend this school the student had to be proficient in German. In South America there were a few elementary schools.

The American Union established its first elementary school in the United States about 1979. It has since fallen apart due to lack of interest from the Union committee members and jealousy on the part of members in other areas where there are no schools. Reformers will seldom send their children to Adventist schools since they believe that these pose a danger to Reform children. This is probably the truth; the children would be able to see that many of the accusations made against the Adventist Church by their parents and leaders are false.

Most Reformers simply give no priority to the education of their children with respect to a Christian setting. This forms no part of their thinking. When they are confronted with the clear statements from the Spirit of Prophecy regarding the importance of Christian education, they simply answer that we are too close to the end of time to establish such schools. As a result, their children are subjected to the non-Christian influences of the public schools.

Problems in Adventist schools provide another excuse for Reformers not operating educational institutions. They reason that public schools are just as good. When a school had been started at the American Union headquarters, every expenditure to expand this project was looked upon as a waste by some members of the union committee. This criticism was made even though little or no operating expense was called for. The church only supplied the building used by the school.

Reformation Study Course

In 1972 the American Union of the Reform Movement (IMS) prepared a series of studies in an attempt to justify its position for being a separate organization. The first lessons of the *Reformation Study Course* were sent to all Adventist workers in the world field with the hope of gaining new converts. It was successful in spreading the work of the movement to a few additional countries, especially to India where there had been no previous work.

It is my understanding that recently a great upheaval has occurred in the work there, due again to arbitrary actions by the General Conference leadership. For this reason it is not possible at this point to know how many members the movement may still have in that country.

The "Reformation Study Course" is filled with many false and misleading assumptions. Let me share just one of these. Lesson 16 carries the following statement:

> As we study the previous angels in Revelation 14, we find that each represented a special group of people with a specific message and with leaders of its own. William Miller led out in the first angel's message, but in the second angel's message he was not so prominent, and in the midnight cry of 1844 he joined only in the very end. *Different leaders took hold of the work each time and carried it forward. Thus the third angel was again a group of people with new leadership, new organization, and a new message. Every new angel brought a shaking and new light.*[8]

The authors make this statement to justify the Reform as a separate movement since they see the Reform as "the other angel of Revelation 18."

Let us now look at what the Spirit of Prophecy says about this:

8 *Reformation Study Course,* Lesson 16 (emphasis added).

> After the passing of the time, God entrusted to His faithful followers the precious principles of present truth. *These principles were not given to those who had no part in the giving of the first and second angels' messages. They were given to the workers who had had a part in the cause from the beginning.*[9]

Here again is an example of how the Reformers distort the history of the Adventist movement in order to prove themselves the people of God.

Fruitage of the Movement

At the 1978 General Conference session the Reform Movement (IMS) claimed a world membership of about 12,000 members, which included an estimated 3,000 in Russia. Later, the figure for Russia was revised downward to about 100 members. In some areas their work has been advancing; in others, declining. In America it has remained static for many years with possibly a small increase for a few years followed by a decline. In 1983, for instance, about 10 percent of the membership in the American Union left the church at approximately the same time. This included about two-thirds of the workers employed by the Union the previous year.

I am not able to give accurate membership figures for the '51 Movement faction. My understanding is that they have a similar number of members as the IMS, or just slightly higher.

Sad to say, the fruits of the Reform Movement do not reveal the special blessing of God upon it. This is certainly not to say that all is bad there. The Lord has faithful souls in the communion of the Reform Movement, people who are ignorant of the facts or who have mistaken notions about certain matters of truth. I have a great deal of compassion and love for these people.

I was once deceived by the Reform teachings, and I pray that the Lord will open the eyes of other members as He has mine. Having been born and reared in the movement, I can say that I honestly believed that what I had been taught was the total truth. My mind was so filled with ill will toward Adventists that anything I witnessed which would cause me to doubt the Reform Movement was looked upon as a temptation from Satan.

Such is the cult spirit that is fostered. It is lamentable but real. Let us pray for these deceived souls. Only the power of the Holy Spirit can break through the prejudice built up over many years. The membership honestly believes that anyone who leaves the Reform will be lost since they must have left the Lord.

---

9 Ellen G. White, *Selected Messages*, book 2 (Washington, DC: Review & Herald Publishing Assn., 1958), p. 389 (emphasis added).

Witnessing the spirit which is in the movement today makes me think of an account I read many years ago. It troubled me then, and continued to do so while I was a member and worker in the Reform. It is the personal experience of Stephen Smith who refused to read a testimony sent him by Ellen White. Instead, he joined several different fringe movements until finally the Holy Spirit softened his heart and he confessed his wrong and was reunited with the remnant church. Part of his confession reads as follows:

> Facts are stubborn things. But the facts are that those who have opposed this work have come to nought, and those who have been in sympathy with it have prospered, have grown better, more devoted and Godlike. *Those who have opposed it have only learned to fight and debate, and they've lost all their religion. No honest man can help seeing that God is with the Advent Movement and against us who have opposed it.* I want to be in fellowship with this people in heart and in the church.[10]

This experience applies all too aptly to the fringe movement under discussion. While it is true that some dear souls have grown spiritually in the Reform Movement, in general the fruits of the leaders and membership are the fruits of criticism, debate, separation, and struggles for power and authority.

The evidence is lacking to show that this movement is "lightening the earth with the heavenly influence" as was prophesied of the reformatory movement spoken of in the Spirit of Prophecy. While the Reformers claim to be the angel of Revelation 18, the facts are that after 73 years of existence they have only a small presence in a few cities in North America and sparse membership in other lands. While Reformers like to believe that Adventist ministers fear them, the reality is that few ministers have ever heard of the Reform Movement.

The entire history of the Reform Movement is a depressing history of struggle due both to persecution from without and more so from troubles within. Even with a very vivid imagination, it is impossible to say that the Lord has shown His rich blessing on this religious movement.

Currently Reformers carry on a small work in many portions of the world. Their stronghold no longer is in Germany where the movement started and where the General Conference of one of the factions (IMS)

10 *Spirit of Prophecy Treasure Chest: An Advent Source Collection of Materials Relating to the Gift of Prophecy in the Remnant Church and the Life and Ministry of Ellen G. White* (Washington, DC: Review & Herald Publishing Assn. for Prophetic Guidance School of the Voice of Prophecy, 1960), p. 48 (emphasis added).

is still located. A larger work has developed in South America, in lands where people are still willing to accept dictatorial control and Roman Catholic concepts of authoritarianism.

In this booklet I speak mostly about the "International Missionary Society" faction of the movement, because I was a member. But what is said here applies to both groups since they have common origins and hold to the same basic teachings. If anything, the other faction of the movement ('51) is even more radical and its leaders even more deceitful than the group of which I was a member.

Reformers still spend much of their time either criticizing the Adventist Church to justify themselves as a separate organization or ridiculing the other faction of the Reform Movement and its people. Such criticism has, sad to say, become their religion.

> Satan is "the accuser of the brethren," and it is his spirit that inspires men to watch for the errors and defects of the Lord's people, and to hold them up to notice, while their good deeds are passed by without a mention.[11]

11 *The Great Controversy,* p. 395.

Chapter 4

One Man's Pilgrimage From Sinai to Calvary

The journey of the children of Israel from Mt. Sinai to the promised land was a long one. Because of unbelief the nation wandered in the wilderness for 40 years. If they had been willing to follow the Lord's instructions, they would have entered the promised land much sooner.

The apostle Paul, in the book of Hebrews, gives insight into the problem. Israel attempted to gain the promised land in the very way others have attempted to gain heaven. They depended upon their own works to earn their deliverance rather than resting in the Lord and His perfect salvation. "For he that is entered into his rest, he also hath ceased from his own works, as God did from his" (Heb 4:10).

Home Years

Many others have made the journey from Sinai to Calvary before, but this story is about my personal journey. I was born in a Christian home where much stress was placed on strict obedience to God and His Word. The penalty for disobedience was clearly portrayed, as was the reward for obedience. I seem to remember more the emphasis on the justice of God rather than the love He has manifested toward the children of men. I came to look upon God the Father as a stern judge—the stern father image—and Jesus as the condescending mother image, the one who protects the child against the overstrictness of the Father.

My purpose for writing is to portray what turned me from an ardent member and worker in the Reform Movement to a member and worker in the Seventh-day Adventist Church. Those who knew me well could not question the fact that before 1982 I was as firm a believer in the authenticity of the Reform Movement as anyone could be.

My parental home was a very exclusive one, not in wealth but in the view that we were the chosen people of God. All outsiders were considered agents of Satan. We children were forbidden to associate with other youngsters lest they, as children of the evil one, should contaminate us.

Since our church had no schools of its own, I attended public school along with my brother and three sisters. We were not permitted to participate in any outside activities. Nor did we engage in the physical education programs within the school. The latter involved competition which my father firmly believed was sinful and forbidden by the Lord.

Consequently I remember feeling myself a stranger among my peers. I had no close friends at any time, even through high school years. I was afraid to associate with others because, after all, it was "us and them"—"the people of God in opposition to the children of the devil." The watchword was always, "be ye separate," in the manner in which the Jewish people kept themselves aloof from the "heathen" around them.

At about age 13 I was baptized into my parent's church, the Seventh-day Adventist Reform Movement (IMS). There was no question in my mind but that this church was the only true people of God. I must be a part of this movement if I wanted to be saved. This had been firmly embedded in my mind since childhood. I had a fairly good understanding of the doctrines of the church, but as I look back, I wonder if I really knew our loving Lord as I should have. Such a relationship was not made as much a priority for acceptance into church membership as was doctrinal understanding.

I was only 11 years old when I witnessed the beginnings of a terrible conflict between two factions of the Reform Movement. On one hand was the American Union, fighting to avoid total domination by the General Conference (IMS) in Germany. On the other hand was the leader who had been sent by the General Conference to force the Union into submission to its will. I viewed this conflict from close proximity since my father was a minister and conference officer of the Reform Movement.

As a result of this conflict, I saw a goodly number of the members of the Reform Movement leave and enter the Seventh-day Adventist Church. Others totally gave up their faith. The battle between the Reformers drained the union treasury and even absorbed a special fund that had been gathered to begin health work in the United States. All the resources of the church were used up in fighting one another instead of giving the last message of warning to the world or expanding the work in other ways.

The struggle between these two factions escalated in 1951, at which time the Reform movement split. D. Nicolici, with a group of supporters, set up his own General Conference and began to battle with the original movement. Now there were two General Conferences of the Reform Movement. Each declared the other to be in rebellion and disfellowshipped one another. Each accused the other of trying to change the "Principles" of the Movement.

This fighting has continued from that day to the present. Whenever one faction establishes a group of believers, the other attempts to gain the new members for themselves.

While the IMS attempted to fight these battles on the basis of the facts of the situation, the other faction distributed documents of accusation against our leaders. Again and again as a young person I was forced to witness a carnal battle being fought by people who made a high profession of godliness, but who were only fighting for their own glory and honor. All too often I witnessed lies being perpetrated by the opposing faction in order to confuse simple people into supporting their organization and leadership.

I had been indoctrinated from earliest childhood to believe that the Reform was totally correct and that the Adventist Church was a totally apostate organization. Whenever anything would take place to shake the confidence of a person (such as the strife for leadership which resulted in the Reform schism in 1951), he was told that this was proof that the movement must be of God. If the Reform were not the work of God, Satan would not try so hard to destroy it.

Later I came to realize that such battles for supremacy were not new in the Reform Movement. It was a nearly continuous fact of life from the very beginning. The struggles were hidden from the people except where this was impossible, such as during the years 1948-1952.

Being closely associated with the work because my father was a minister in the movement, I was not totally ignorant of what was going on. At the same time to express questions about the direction the movement was heading was considered sinful. It implied doubt that the Lord was leading. After all, since the Adventist Church was held to be "a fallen church," where else could a person go?

It is only natural that people in fringe movements separating from the Adventist Church (such as the Reform Movement) should have most of their contacts with others of a similar persuasion. They may also have some things in common with those who have experienced personal grievances in the Adventist Church. Looking back at many of the reports that were circulated among us Reform members, I realize now that they were seriously distorted by the sources which brought them.

As children we were taught to look with suspicion upon anything done by the leaders and people of the "mother church." Everything which they did and wrote must be distorted. Had they not placed themselves on the side of Satan by "overthrowing the original position of the pioneers"? Eventually I discovered that we did not even know the original position of the pioneers. In reality the Reformers, consciously or unconsciously, were trying to rewrite Adventist history to suit their own ideas of how it should have been.

Service in the Reform Movement

After completing high school and working for a few years as an architectural draftsman, I felt the call of the Lord to enter missionary service. I was convinced that the Lord's coming could not be too far off. As I saw the smallness of the Reform Movement and realized how much work needed to be done to warn a world still lying in darkness, I saw a need of doing my part in hastening the coming of the Lord.

I first began working on a part-time basis as a literature evangelist. Since the only missionary school the Reform Movement had was in Germany (with instruction only in German), I obtained my training in the school of experience—through literature evangelism and giving Bible studies to contacts. In addition, I obtained some training from working with more experienced workers in the field. After I began working full-time in missionary outreach, the American Union instituted seminars to give additional training to its workers.

My wife and I were married in 1962 and began working together to win souls for the Lord, or to the church (to the minds of Reformers the two are synonymous). We became skillful in giving Bible studies on doctrinal matters. But we were never taught how to bring a soul to the foot of the cross. As a result, we won very few persons. Subsequent to these labors we responded to an appointment to do full-time missionary service in Richmond, Virginia. Here, to a great extent, my pilgrimage began in earnest.

As I worked from door to door, I frequently faced the question posed by some of those dear Southern Baptists: "Are you saved?" This was an important question to them. However, I could not give a clear, honest answer. My inner response was, I hope to be, or If I am faithful, I will be, or I'm working on it. Within my heart I knew that such an answer would not be acceptable to these earnest people, nor were such answers acceptable to myself. This dilemma took me to the Scriptures and the Spirit of Prophecy for answers. As I studied, it began to dawn in my darkened mind that while I could not accept the Baptist view of "once saved, always saved," as a child of God I could and I must have the assurance of salvation today.

It took the children of Israel many years to travel to the promised land. My pilgrimage likewise took many years. Step by step through much study and the Lord's leading, the process went forward in my life. While working with the local Reform Church in Richmond, I was able to experience firsthand the terrible results of legalism. Members whom I knew were not by any stretch of the imagination living the Christian life were very strong in obeying the letter of the law and condemning those who did not see things as they did.

After being ordained to the ministry, I was transferred to Canada to take over a district of three churches. There I found a membership divided down the middle over legalistic views. At times I had to sit in committee meetings until 2:00 a.m. listening to accusations against church members and demands to punish them. For example, a member who popped popcorn on Sabbath afternoon should be "dealt with." Should members be permitted to own a television set? Was the organist's hair long enough? Should she be removed from office because she had her hair cut? I began to see the real calamity of legalism. I saw churches and families torn apart by unchristian actions, all in the name of doing "God's will." This intensified my desire for something better.

In the meantime I continued fulfilling my task as well as I could. This led me to visit the prayer meeting of the Adventist Church in order to find persons I could interest in the Reform Movement. I did not obtain any converts in this manner, but I did see many things about the Adventist Church which I came to admire. In one church the pastor conducted witnessing classes from which I learned how to bring the message of salvation to people more effectively. As I employed these principles, my ministry slowly began to bear fruit, and souls were won to Christ as well as to the church.

In my study I came to gain clearer views of the message of justification by faith as presented by the brethren Jones and Waggoner to the Adventist Church in 1888. But my past indoctrination in the Reform's teaching prejudiced me to believe that this wonderful message had been rejected by the Adventist Church. That's why, I had been taught, there was a need for the Reform Movement.

I did at times have some doubts as to the reality of this "rejection." It seemed to me that the message was being proclaimed more clearly by the Adventist Church than by the Reform Movement. In my mind there still was no question that the Reform Movement embraced the people of God. Fulfilling my "duty" as a good Reformer, I looked for every sign of apostasy in my contacts with the "mother church." When I witnessed problems in the Reform Movement, it just confirmed my conviction that this must be the people of God or else Satan would not be so angry and attempt to destroy the Movement. Only vaguely did the thought enter my mind that just possibly we were building on a foundation of the sand of human devisings.

While working in Canada and the eastern portion of the United States, I had to do battle with the workers of the rebel faction ('51) time and again. On one occasion I found it necessary to spend several days in Boston and New York debating with some of their leaders because they were attempting to take over the members of our group.

While I realized that the leaders of the IMS I represented were not perfect, the strength of my argument was that at least they did not try to deceive the people. I witnessed again and again the terrible propensity of the leaders of this rebel group to lie and twist the facts in order to try to win an argument. Up to that time I had never witnessed the same weakness in the leaders of my group. This was soon to change.

While working in California during the years 1975-1977, I helped establish a new group which later organized into a church. Then in 1977 I accepted a call to serve as American Union president (IMS) in Denver, Colorado. The next year (1978) I was elected to serve as North American Division president as well. These heavy responsibilities kept me away from my family for extended periods. My wife assumed the extra burden of rearing our two teenage children in the absence of a husband/father while working full time in the publishing office.

The new challenges, however, were stimulating, and I put my full energy into making these fields into effective entities. At the outset I was told by the leaders of the General Conference (IMS) that these were "sick fields" which needed to be reorganized completely. I found the sickness to be much more than skin deep or just organizational.

The entire Mexican and Central American Reform Movement (IMS) was racked by legalism and corruption. Souls were not cared for by loving shepherds, but were whipped into submission by uncaring minidictators. Leaders held the church properties in their own private names, and, in a few instances, lived as kings while the members existed in poverty. Members were disfellowshipped or put on discipline for no greater reason than starting a health work as a lay endeavor without the permission of the church leader.

I worked hard to turn the tide of corruption in these areas only to find later that similar things were being done on the General Conference level. As a member of the General Conference Committee, I soon discovered that tithe funds were being used for other purposes than the messenger of the Lord stated. Instead of providing support for missionary workers, the tithe was being used to purchase properties in various parts of the world. All this was taking place without the approval, or even the knowledge, of the General Conference Committee.

Offerings gathered for special purposes were not allocated for those stated purposes but were disbursed according to the whims of the president and treasurer. In order to obtain any funds previously allocated to a project in your area, it was necessary to be in their good graces.

I protested such action and stated that the membership would not agree with this practice of diverting funds from the purpose for which they were given. I was informed that it was not the business of members to know how funds were being disbursed. For the first time I experienced my own leaders and co-workers purposely fabricating falsehoods. This greatly disillusioned me, and doubts began to surface in regard to the genuineness of the movement.

It soon became clear that the goal of the leaders of the General Conference (IMS) was to replace the local minidictators in the world field with their own authority. They demanded, for instance, that every church property in Central America be deeded over to the General Conference (IMS) with the president and treasurer as acting administrators. I found that this had been done already in South America and Puerto Rico.

As division president I resisted such moves. I was convinced that in the event of a Communist takeover in any of these countries, the very first properties which would be confiscated would be those owned by foreign organizations. The Central American Union Committee fully agreed with this position and refused to yield to these improper, arbitrary demands.

Later when the American Union, with the encouragement of the General Conference (IMS), purchased land to establish a health work in the United States, the financial help which had been promised previously was then made contingent upon this property being signed over to the General Conference. This situation made me aware of the dangerous path the Reform leadership was taking in establishing "kingly power" against which Ellen White had warned so strongly.

As I turned to the Spirit of Prophecy for enlightenment, some very pointed statements showed that a similar situation had taken place years ago in the Adventist Church. The servant of the Lord had spoken out in opposition to such a situation.

> When it is deemed expedient to invest means in school buildings, in sanitariums, or in homes for the poor in any country, in order to establish the work there, the Lord would have those who are living in that locality walk humbly before Him, and to show that they realize their personal dependence upon Him, and that they believe in His willingness to help them to plan, to devise, to arrange intelligently for His work. He is as willing to give wisdom to those who feel the value of divine grace, as to give wisdom to some other mind, who will then, at great expense, communicate the same to you. Where is your faith? Will men turn from the God of wisdom to seek wisdom from finite men, sending for men from a long distance to come and help them out of perplexity? How does the Lord look upon this?[1]

---

1 *Testimonies to Ministers,* p. 324.

Doctrinal Differences

It was only after I was elected to serve as president of the North American Division and as a member of the General Conference Committee of the Reform Movement (IMS) that I began to see serious problems in the organization. First of all, I began to see doctrinal differences between what I had learned from Reform leaders in America (and my own study of the Bible and *Testimonies*) and what was taught by the European leaders. I very quickly began to note the dishonesty of some leaders in the day-to-day operation of the organization. This made me wonder if deception was practiced in other areas as well.

I had realized for many years that the movement had problems with the "Principles" booklet which lays down the movement's "Fundamental Beliefs." Most of the workers and many members realized that there were matters in this booklet which did not agree with the clear statements of the Bible and the writings of the prophet of God. Still everyone was afraid to correct this booklet for fear that the opposition Reform Movement (the '51 faction) would use such changes to its advantage. Their leaders would then be able to say that we had changed, so they could claim to be the original movement, those who held to the founding beliefs of the Reform.

Despite this fear, the delegates of the General Conference (IMS) voted in 1978 to rewrite the booklet. When the General Conference Committee attempted to begin this work, however, it quickly became apparent that any correction or change would be impossible. In pondering this impasse, I once again turned to the Bible and especially the Spirit of Prophecy to see what the servant of the Lord had to say in such matters.

In my heart I asked the question, Lord, how have we gotten ourselves into such a dead-end situation in which we know that our fundamental statement of faith is incorrect, and yet we are not able to change it? What I found in the Spirit of Prophecy startled me. Before this time I never questioned the need for our doctrinal statement. All at once I realized that the Reform Movement, which I loved dearly, had fallen into a trap of Satan by establishing an immovable creed. A "thus saith the Lord" had been replaced by a "thus saith the church" in direct opposition to the instruction of the Lord. The following statements made me take a second look at what I had been previously taught.

> There are many at the present day thus clinging to the customs and traditions of their fathers. When the Lord sends them additional light, they refuse to accept it, because, not having been granted to their fathers, it was not received by them. We are not placed where our fathers were; consequently our duties

> and responsibilities are not the same as theirs. We shall not be approved of God in looking to the example of our fathers to determine our duty instead of searching the word of truth for ourselves. Our responsibility is greater than was that of our ancestors. We are accountable for the light which they received, and which was handed down as an inheritance for us, and we are accountable also for the additional light which is now shining upon us from the word of God.[2]
>
> But God will have a people upon the earth to maintain the Bible, and the Bible only, as the standard of all doctrines and the basis of all reforms. The opinions of learned men, the deductions of science, the creeds or decisions of ecclesiastical councils, as numerous and discordant as are the churches which they represent, the voice of the majority—not one nor all of these should be regarded as evidence for or against any point of religious faith. *Before accepting any doctrine or precept, we should demand a plain "Thus saith the Lord"* in its support.[3]

The Roman Church advocates the concept that the church has the right to determine doctrine in spite of what the Word of God may say. In opposition to this position is the Protestant insistence that all doctrine must be based on the Bible and the Bible only. I came to the realization that the Reform Movement holds to the Catholic view of this matter, rather than to the Protestant view.

The Reform teaches that the church has authority to enact religious legislation, despite clear statements to the contrary by the Bible and Spirit of Prophecy. For example, the Reform Movement has made the question of vegetarianism a test of fellowship, despite the clear statement from the Pen of Inspiration that no such position should be taken: "We are not to make the use of flesh food a test of fellowship."[4] Reformers excuse their position by claiming that light has progressed to the place where the previous statement is no longer applicable. As difficult as it may be for Reformers to admit, their attitudes toward church authority are more Catholic than Protestant.

I began to realize that the Reform was filled with many man-made rules. The Word of God takes second place to a "thus saith the church." When this fact began to sink in, I realized something was essentially wrong with the movement which I loved and to which I had given 20 years of my life.

---

2 *The Great Controversy,* p. 164.
3 Ibid., p. 595 (emphasis added).
4 *Testimonies for the Church,* 9:159.

One evening I attended an evangelistic meeting in an Adventist Church close to my home in Colorado. The film "Deceived" was shown. This film documents the history of Jim Jones and Jonestown. It caused me to do a great deal of sober thinking. It pointed out that when the "People's Temple" first began, it seemed to be a place where the love of Christ shone out. The members engaged in a great work to reach out to assist their fellowmen. People were drawn to this church because of the fellowship and blessings they received.

However, the situation changed as Jim Jones gradually became a dictator over the people. We now know the final result of such brainwashing. The news media revealed the horror when several hundred people blindly followed their leader to their deaths. As I viewed this film, the frightening realization came to me that many similar situations were taking place in the church which was my life. Could it be that my church, begun for a good cause, had been sidetracked and was headed in a similar direction as "People's Temple"? This experience caused me to search out what the Lord truly desired His church to be.

Around the same time the Lord placed in my hands several books which further aroused my thinking. In 1981 the Adventists published the "Early Elmshaven Years" (volume 5 in a 6 volume biography of Ellen G. White). As I read this book, I reviewed the experiences through which the Adventist Church had passed in those days. I realized that the Reform had in its midst the very same problems against which Ellen White had spoken so strongly. One day while visiting in California, I browsed around the Adventist Book Center and came upon a book on Adventist history, "Light Bearers to the Remnant," by R. W. Schwarz. I purchased this book with the intent of using material in it against the Adventist Church. It documented many things of which I was never aware before.

On another occasion, while visiting relatives in Berrien Springs, Michigan, I purchased another book which documented the fallacy of the idea that the message of justification by faith had been rejected by the Adventist Church in 1888. This book, *Thirteen Crisis Years,* by Elder A. V. Olson, reveals the fact that even though many of the leading men did reject the message at first, they later repented and accepted it. Additionally, the fact is that the church did not take any official action on this subject in 1888.

I now saw the Reform claim—that this heaven-sent message was rejected and as a result the Reform Movement was born—was false. Thus their claim to be represented by the angel of Revelation 18 could have no basis in fact. I realized that it was actually the Reformers who were holding to the teachings and attitudes which had brought about the need for this message. They had never accepted the message themselves; neither did they understand it.

As I began to grasp these new ideas, I felt duty bound to share this knowledge with my fellow believers. It was clear that we had taken a false road. It was my desire to help the people to see what needed correcting so we could place ourselves in the position where the Lord desired us to be.

I attempted to change the direction of the movement by appealing to the members of the General Conference Committee, but without success. I wrote and spoke out against the many wrong positions held by the movement which my study of the Spirit of Prophecy had revealed. In the end, however, I was finally forced to realize that to be true to the Bible and Spirit of Prophecy I must separate myself from such a false movement.

There had been a great deal of controversy between me and the leaders of the Reform General Conference (IMS), especially in regard to the use of monies. First, the leadership believed that the people had no right to know how the tithes and offerings were being used. Secondly, they expected my salary and expenses for travel to every part of the North American Division to be paid by the American Union. At the same time they were collecting funds from every part of the division and not passing them back to that division. I had no budget for operations until I pressed the General Conference leaders to the limit. It was then voted that I would receive such a budget, but it never arrived.

As a final straw, they allowed the former leaders in Mexico to take over the union again after the delegates had voted them out of office and revoked their credentials. This was done despite the fact that the General Conference leadership itself had previously declared these men to be corrupt and no longer worthy of any office in the church. As a result, I resigned as division president at the end of December 1981 but continued on as American Union president.

Since the General Conference (IMS) leadership now realized that I was not a yes-man, they were determined to get rid of me. In response to a letter I had written to the General Conference president I received a short note from him which, among other things, simply quoted a Bible text, "And the man that will do presumptuously, and will not hearken unto the priest that standeth to minister before the Lord thy God, or unto the judge, even that man shall die: and thou shalt put away the evil from Israel" (Deut. 17:12). I realized that this was a pronouncement of judgment by the president against me. Later events proved this to be true.

In the Spring of 1982 I wrote a small booklet, "Our Commission," in which I pointed out some of the problems I saw in the Reform Movement. This booklet was composed mostly of statements from the Pen of Inspiration. In writing this booklet I realized full well that some would not like what was set forth. Before publication the manuscript had been read by all but one member of the American Union Literature Committee. They agreed that it should be printed, not as an official church publication, but simply as coming from me, a church leader.

The booklet raised the ire of some members of the church, especially the General Conference leadership. At a district conference in Pennsylvania in August 1982 the General Conference leaders demanded that I retract everything said in the booklet and then suffer the punishment due for writing it. I asked to be shown my error and assured them I would retract what I had written if I could be shown the deviation from the Bible and *Testimonies.* Only one brother even attempted to show me an error. What he considered improper was in reality nothing more than a paraphrase of several Bible texts.

From August until December of that year I did much praying and studying. I began to reexamine some of the differences between the teachings of the Reform and the Adventist Church. I became convinced that when the doctrinal differences are studied without prejudice, accepting only what is written in the Word of God, the teachings of the Adventist Church are more correct.

Separation

It still was not possible for me to think that the movement which I had so strongly supported was not the true people of God. I believed that they had just strayed away but would be called back by the Lord. I prayed earnestly to the Lord that if the Reform were not the people of God, He would clearly show me by the spirit revealed in the delegates' meetings of the union conference in California. The session was to take place in December. I asked the Lord to reveal to me personally the true nature of the movement. In every way possible I tried to work for peace in these meetings without sacrificing principle.

The Lord made it very plain to me that there was a false, satanic spirit in the meeting. There was a spirit I had never before experienced. At one point I had stepped out of the meetings to speak for a moment to the General Conference president about some concerns which I had, and two of the delegates came out screaming like demons because their way had been crossed. At this point I realized that my prayers had been answered. Just as Martin Luther rose from the steps of "Pilate's staircase" and hastened from Rome (see *The Great Controversy,* p. 125), I found it necessary to withdraw from the Reform Movement. Still, I received repeated appeals to remain as a pastor of the Denver, Colorado, Reform Church.

In December 1982 my wife and I resigned from every office in the Reform Movement, as did several other workers in the American Union. This was an act of faith on our part and was done against the advice of friends. My dear wife, who stood faithfully at my side through all this turmoil, had held the important position of coordinating the publishing house in the American Union.

Our friends advised us to continue on in the movement, even though we did not believe that it was the people of God, until we could find other employment. This we could not do conscientiously. Since we could no longer pay a faithful tithe to such an organization, we could not accept payment from the tithes either. Praise be to the Lord who took care of us during those first trying months! He never allowed us to go hungry despite six months with no income.

After severing employment with the Reform Movement, I began to study in earnest, reviewing in detail the differences between the teachings of the Reform Movement and the Adventist Church. I realized that others in the Movement were still looking to me for spiritual leadership. My studies were conducted now in a different manner than before. As a Reformer, I would go to the Word of God with the desire to prove my position correct. Now I went to the Word, asking the Lord to remove all my preconceived ideas and to reveal His truth to me. This brought me to the realization that the teachings of the Adventist Church, which I had fought against all these years, were correct and my previous concepts false.

My mind, however, found it difficult to overcome the indoctrination of many years against the Adventist Church. As Reformers, we saw the Adventist Church as being in a "terrible apostate condition." I now wanted to know how the teachings were put into practice.

I began to visit the Adventist Church in Littleton, Colorado. What I witnessed there convinced me that from childhood I had been greatly misinformed about this movement which God has called to give His message for the last days. I realized that this was the place to where the Lord desired to lead me. The Lord worked in such a way that my wife and children also began to visit the Adventist Church. Soon, as a family, we were accepted as members. As my wife and I studied the Adventist "Fundamental Beliefs," we found the truth we had believed in for years.

Through the love and consideration of some pastors and leaders in the Adventist Church, I once again received the opportunity to work for the Lord on a full-time basis. I never cease to marvel at the loving acceptance shown us, former enemies to the cause of the Lord. Never have we been made to feel as enemies or in any way looked down upon or criticized.

Now I praise the Lord for the opportunity to preach the Bible's message without being forced to teach man-made requirements. As souls are brought to the foot of the cross, it is beautiful to witness what the Holy Spirit does in their lives. In the Reform we felt that we must do the work of the Holy Spirit by pressing upon the people the requirements of the church. But we have come to realize that the Lord is able to do the work of transforming lives Himself.

I am so thankful for the leading of the Lord in my pilgrimage from the legalism of Sinai to freedom in Christ. Lest some mistake the meaning of such freedom, it should be said that this freedom is not a license for transgression, but makes possible an even closer, more obedient walk with the Lord. It is freedom from the oppression of human rules and regulations. It is accepting God's Word, including the messages given through the prophetic gift, as being applicable to me personally and resisting the urge to make it fit others only.

I encourage those who may read this experience, if they are still standing at the foot of Sinai, to take the trip to Calvary. The Lord will lead you on this journey as He did me. Cast off the shackles of legalism and find the true joy of serving the Lord!

Chapter 5

Mistaken Concepts—Part 1

In order to relate effectively to members of the Seventh-day Adventist Reform Movement, it is necessary to be aware of the concepts which affect their thinking.

Spirit of Pharisaism

First and foremost is their concept of a vengeful God who is ready to destroy anyone who steps out of line. Consequently they insist that the unfaithfulness of the European church leaders during World War I disqualified them as workers for God. But the Reformers reason even further: Since the Adventist Church leaders made this terrible mistake in the war, God has rejected *the entire church.* As new leaders, the Reformers believe that they have been called to carry forward the work of the Lord.

This view of things distorts and misrepresents the character of the God we serve. It strikingly contrasts with the portrayal of the merciful God revealed in both the Old and New Testaments and especially in the life of Jesus. Jesus reprimanded the disciples who desired to call fire from heaven upon those who had rejected Him.

We may consider the patience God exercised toward ancient Israel, despite the fact that they rebelled against Him again and again. Their entire history is one continuous fluctuation from apostasy to reform and again to flagrant apostasy. These times of apostasy were punctuated with examples of remedial judgments from God for their sins. But final rejection did not come until after hundreds of years and after every possible effort on the part of God had failed to bring them to repentance.

Babylonian captivity resulted from years of evil. They worshipped images and offered their own children as human sacrifices. Despite such terrible actions, the long-suffering God we serve gave them yet another chance. He continued to search for His people as a shepherd searches for a lost sheep. This love was the opposite of the rabbinical concept.

> The rabbis had a saying that there is rejoicing in heaven when one who has sinned against God is destroyed; but Jesus taught

> that to God the work of destruction is a strange work. That in which all heaven delights is the restoration of God's own image in the souls whom He has made.[1]

After the close of World War I, the Adventist brethren in Europe were confronted with the fact that their attitude toward military service was not in harmony with the traditional Adventist position. "During the subsequent workers' meeting the three SDA leaders who had made the declaration publicly acknowledged that they had made an error and expressed their sincere regret for having done so."[2]

Regarding this confession recorded in the *SDA Encyclopedia,* a later writer for the Reform Movement makes the following comment:

> Now take notice! This confession was "subsequently" made in a worker's meeting, which indicates that it was made among themselves, not before those whom they had so terribly wronged. This is just like a robber, who during a holdup shoots and maims a store owner, feels sorry afterward, and makes full confession to his own family. Does this set things in order again? Is the guilt now wiped out and forgotten? Of course not! *If no restitution is made, his confession to his family is null and void. At Friedensau, in 1920, no attempt was made to recommend the few who stood faithful for their conviction and who suffered and died for it. Nothing was made good; nothing was reinstated; nothing was corrected.*[3]

Note that the Reformer's main concern is that they should have been honored for their faithfulness, while the leaders who had been in error should have been pushed into the ground. This fulfills the attitude of the Pharisee as described by Ellen White.

> When one who has wandered far in sin seeks to return to God, he will encounter criticism and distrust. There are those who will doubt whether his repentance is genuine, or will whisper, "He has no stability; I do not believe that he will hold out." These persons are doing not the work of God but the work of Satan, who is the accuser of the brethren. Through their

1 Ellen G. White, *Christ's Object Lessons* (Washington, DC: Review & Herald Publishing Assn., 1941), p. 190.

2 *SDA Encyclopedia,* Commentary Reference Series, vol. 10, art. "SDA Reform Movement," rev. ed. (Washington, DC: Review & Herald Publishing Assn., 1976), p. 1333.

3 *Commenting on the Commentary* (International Missionary Society, Seventh-day Adventist Reform Movement).

> criticisms the wicked one hopes to discourage that soul, and to drive him still farther from hope and from God.[4]

The God we serve takes delight in forgiving the sinner. "Who is a God like unto thee, that pardoneth iniquity, and passeth by the transgression of the remnant of his heritage? he retaineth not his anger for ever, because he delighteth in mercy" (Mic 7:18).

> These souls whom you despise, said Jesus, are the property of God. By creation and by redemption they are His, and they are of value in His sight. As the shepherd loves his sheep, and cannot rest if even one be missing, so, in an infinitely higher degree, does God love every outcast soul. Men may deny the claim of His love, they may wander from Him, they may choose another master; yet they are God's, and He longs to recover His own.[5]

If the early Reformers had had such love for the erring, they would have desired restoration rather than punishment of the brethren.

Attitudes Toward Military Service

Another mistaken concept held by Reformers pertains to the position the Adventist pioneers took concerning military service at the time of the American Civil War. The Reformers are convinced that the pioneers opposed any kind of participation in the military during that war. They believe that the Adventist pioneers had no question what the true position should be.

This matter is so simple to the Reformers that they feel no true believer could participate in any kind of military service, even in medical work. The history of this matter, however, discloses a different picture. The Adventist pioneers actually found this problem very difficult to resolve properly.

It is not within the scope of this section to go into detail regarding the matter, but it is important to get a general overview of the discussion which took place during that terrible Civil War.

Reformers regard the statement in *Testimonies for the Church,* vol. 1, p. 361, as the final and only position regarding military service at all times and in all places. But they overlook many other important factors.

> I was shown that God's people, who are His peculiar treasure, cannot engage in this perplexing war, for it is opposed to every

4 *Christ's Object Lessons,* p. 190.
5 Ibid., p. 187.

> principle of their faith. In the army they cannot obey the truth and at the same time obey the requirements of their officers. There would be a continual violation of conscience.[6]

In taking this statement literally, they overlook and rationalize the expression, "this perplexing war." Neglecting to find out what is meant by the phrase, Reformers reason that since the purpose of the Civil War was to free the slaves, it must have been a war more just than most. This being the case, they argue, the statement applies even more forcefully to other war situations as well as to peacetime draft. Other statements in the same chapter are overlooked. These reveal why this war was so perplexing.

> Information sent by our generals to Washington concerning the movement of our armies might nearly as well be telegraphed directly to the rebel forces. There are rebel sympathizers right in the heart of the Union authorities. *This war is unlike any other.* The great lack of union of feeling and action makes it look dark and discouraging. Many of the soldiers have thrown off restraint and have sunk to an alarming state of degradation. How can God go forth with such a corrupt army? How can He, according to His honor, defeat their enemies and lead them on to victory? There is discord, and strife for honor, while the poor soldiers are dying by thousands on the battlefield or from their wounds and from exposure and hardships.
>
> This war is a most singular and at the same time a most horrible and heartsickening conflict. Other nations are looking on with disgust at the transactions of the armies of both North and South. They see such a determined effort to protract the war at an enormous sacrifice of life and money, while at the same time nothing is really gained, that it looks to them like a strife to see which can kill the most men. They are indignant.[7]

The servant of the Lord pointed out the terrible fact that the generals of the North were in sympathy with the principle of slavery and were not really trying to bring an end to this great sin. This was one reason the Adventist believers did not take greater interest in the conflict.

When the Civil War began on May 24, 1861, people expected the conflict to pass quickly. Most Advent believers gave very little thought to the possibility of having to face the issue of military service. Military ranks were being made up largely by volunteers. Adventists were so busy proclaiming

6 *Testimonies for the Church,* 1:361.
7 Ibid., p. 367 (emphasis added).

the soon return of the Lord that they saw the war only as a sign of the last days. A few months after the beginning of the conflict, in October, 1861, Seventh-day Adventists organized their first conference.

As the war continued and more men were lost, it became apparent that the struggle would be protracted. Before long the service was running out of volunteers, and the country recognized the need to conscript troops. This new event caused Advent believers to sit up and take notice. They began to question what position they should take if a draft were enacted.

In the *Review and Herald,* August 12, 1862, James White wrote an article entitled, "The Nation," in which he took up the matter of the proposed draft. He stated that those Adventists who voted in the previous election "to a man voted for Abraham Lincoln." He then proceeded to make a statement which caused a great deal of discussion among the believers.

White observed that the people believed strongly in the sacredness of the law of God, a code which was "not in harmony with all the requirements of war." He then stated,

> But in the case of drafting, the government assumes the responsibility of the violation of the law of God, and it would be madness to resist. He who would resist until, in the administration of military law, he was shot down, goes too far, we think, in taking the responsibility of suicide.[8]

This position raised a storm of protest from some brethren, but others gave it thoughtful consideration. Elder White did not look upon his position as being the last word on the issue. In the September 16 edition of the *Review and Herald,* he stated his object was, "if possible, to check the fanatical rashness which many are liable to run into, and disgrace the cause of truth." He added, "One thing is certain, true believers in the third message would make poor soldiers, unless they first lost the spirit of truth."

Elder White and others were perplexed over what stand to take. He requested others to address themselves to the issue.

> We have spoken frankly upon some points, and would now invite brethren S. Pierce, Hutchins, O. Nichols, Bourdeaus, Cornell, Andrews, Aldrich, Waggoner, Loughborough, Hull, Ingraham, Snook, Brinkerhoof, or any others, to give the brethren light upon the subject.[9]

Several of these brethren did address this, as well as the matter of paying for exemption. J. H. Waggoner wrote,

8 James White, "The Nation," *Review and Herald* (August 12, 1862).
9 "Our Duty in Reference to the War," *The Review and Herald* (September 16, 1862).

> My present conviction is that I would sooner suffer the result of a draft, and trust in God for the consequences, then to accept a $100.00 valuation of my conscience. . . . Not over one in one hundred, if so many, could avail themselves of its provisions, while the poor, the great mass of our brethren, whose consciences are as tender and as valuable as those of the rich, stand precisely where they would stand without it.[10]

Others spoke out even more strongly:

> Shall the Christian, then, who is so greatly indebted to the government for its sheltering care in the past, shall the Christian forsake his country in her hour of peril? Think of it. Is it murder to hang or shoot a traitor? No! no! When men rebel against just and good laws, death is their just due, and the executioner is clear. Does not the army of Mr. Lincoln stand between us and a military despotism worse than Pharaoh's? Shall we, then, shrink from the requisition of a military draft? Are we Christians, yet have no love to the country that has fostered us? I much like Br. White's remarks on this point. We would not shame the memory of Washington and other heroes whom God blessed upon the field of battle. . . .
>
> But while engaged in a crusade against traitors, let us like good and true men, render strict obedience to the laws.[11]

Another writer stated, "But this war does not have as its object directly the extermination of slavery; if it did, I should not object to fighting."[12] Another leading brother stated:

> I do not understand that civilized warfare, or capital punishment, are against the sixth commandment. . . . We should do all we can to avoid breaking God's holy law. If we do this, we shall not willingly place ourselves where we cannot keep the Sabbath, that we may avoid being drafted, and that we may get greater wages. Bro. White's remarks on the condition of drafted Sabbath-keepers are satisfactory to my mind, and I mean to abide by them till I have reasons to believe that they are not correct.[13]

It seems that the point some of the brethren tried to impress upon the

---

10 J. H. Waggoner, "Our Duty and the Nation," *The Review and Herald* (September 23, 1862).
11 Joseph Clarke, "The Sword vs. Fanaticism," *The Review and Herald* (September 23, 1862).
12 J. N. Loughborough, "Do Violence to No Man," *The Review and Herald* (September 30, 1862).
13 D. T. Bordeau, "The Present War," *The Review and Herald* (October 14, 1862).

people was that to volunteer would be wrong, but to accept a draft would be a different matter. There was also concern that the present situation could cause a rift among the Advent believers.

Another writer said,

> There is no necessity for brethren to go to war with each other on *peace principles* [writer's emphasis]. We desire light, however, upon our duty—the true light—and we reasonably expect to have it. . . . It is by no means certain that a man's life would be taken because he declined fighting for conscience' sake. But if every remonstrance failed, and it was evidently coming to this, I would recommend following the advice given, until further light is elicited from the word, or given from above. . . . I want the true light upon the question, and I believe we shall have it.[14]

It is beautiful to see how many of the brethren had open minds to study these matters and even to reconsider their ideas when it seemed that there was light in a certain direction. Consider the following reasoning on the part of one brother:

> Almost from my youth up, I believed that all kinds of war were contrary to the teachings of the New Testament. But after much prayer and serious investigation I now believe that I occupied an extreme position. I am forced to the conclusion that the doctrine of universal non-resistance is an untenable extreme.

Going further he uses the example of Nehemiah in defending Jerusalem from its enemies:

> This testimony proves that fighting in self defense was authorized by God. And where, I ask, has he ever said to the reverse? Nowhere. God has never said that we should stand still and be murdered, or see our families slaughtered by the cruel hands of unholy and ungodly rebels. As the present war of our nation is for self defense, there certainly can be no wrong in aiding to crush the rebels who are trying to overthrow it. . . .
>
> If God allows the lot to fall upon us, let us go and fight in His name.[15]

Elder White did not fully agree with this position as can be seen by his statement, "Brethren Bourdeau and Cottrell, in this week's Review, speak

14 R. F. Cottrell, "Non-resistance," *The Review and Herald* (October 14, 1862).
15 B. F. Snook, "The War and Our Duty," *The Review and Herald* (October 14, 1862).

with wisdom, we think, on the war question. We fear Brn. Snook and Waggoner are tending to the other extreme."[16] However, White did not refuse to print the convictions of these brethren.

Another brother warned against taking any extreme position:

> In regard to the duty of Sabbath-keepers relative to the present war, extremes should be avoided. The cause of the North is just, but there are too many Achans in the camp. The pride of the nation is being humbled. "Tekel" is written upon this government's prosperity, and we look for troublous times.
>
> There are some very serious objections to a voluntary service in this war. . . . Without a special revelation from heaven, it seems like madness and presumption to attempt to resist the authorities. In one case two hundred armed men in Indiana united to resist the draft, but they were overpowered, and in disgrace had to submit.[17]

Needless to say, not all agreed with the position of Brother White. Henry E. Carver took issue with him:

> But, says Bro. White, "In case of drafting, the government assumes the responsibility of violating the law of God." This seems to me to be untenable and dangerous ground; for if the government can assume the responsibility now for the violation of two of those holy precepts, and we go clear, why may not the same government assume the responsibility for the violation of the Sabbath law and we go clear when the edict goes forth that all shall observe the first day of the week?[18]

In the same issue of the *Review and Herald,* James White answered some of the arguments of Brother Carver but then quickly added,

> We have advised no man to go to war. We have struck at that fanaticism which grows out of extreme non-resistance, and have labored to lead our people to seek the Lord and trust Him for deliverance. How this can and will come, we have no light at the present.[19]

Some of the Sabbath-keepers were confused as to what to do under the existing conditions. Brother Martin Kittle wrote to Brother White:

---

16 James White, "The War Question," *The Review and Herald* (October 14, 1862).
17 M. E. Cornell, "Extremes," *The Review and Herald* (October 21, 1862).
18 Henry Carver, "The War," *The Review and Herald* (October 21, 1862).
19 James White, "Letter to Bro. Carver," *The Review and Herald* (October 21, 1862).

> I have been drafted into the United States service. . . . I did think it wrong to go to war; but the pieces in the Review on that subject changed my mind, and made duty look clear.[20]

Stephen Pierce reasoned,

> Think not by this that a spirit of war should be cherished; it should all be subdued from our hearts. And if called upon we should engage in it, as the most painful or revolting duty. Otherwise we shall meet the doom of the transgressor. "Since thou hast not hated blood, even blood shall pursue thee" Eze. 25:6.[21]

0. Nichols took issue with some of the previously published arguments by stating that our present condition cannot be compared with that of the Old Testament. He wrote:

> The gospel of Christ is a new dispensation. . . . The war has dragged on for more than a year-and-a-half. The country has given the government over a million of men, and all the money they could possibly use; yet we have not made scarcely any progress toward crushing the rebellion. The rebel armies still menace the capital; their privateers defy our navy. During this period we have disabled and lost nearly four hundred thousand of our men. It is evident that God is against our armies and is overruling this war for the chastisement of our nation. Should our people who believe Christ's coming is "even at the doors," engage in this war?[22]

Some brethren tried to steer a course of reconciliation between the different opinions. J. M. Aldrich wrote:

> I am still inclined to stand on the no-fight side of the question. But in taking such a position, I desire to say that I would wish to be divested of all fanaticism, and would not, in my relations with the world, exercise undue zeal in the matter. . . . Notwithstanding all that has been said, pro and con, about resisting a draft, I am inclined to think that our discrepancy of views is more apparent than real.

After speaking about the experience of the three Hebrew worthies in Babylon, he said:

---

20 Martin Kittle, "From Bro. Kittle," *The Review and Herald* (October 21, 1862).
21 Stephen Pierce, "Obligation to Human Governments," *The Review and Herald* (October 28, 1862).
22 O. Nichols, "Our Duty Relative to the War," *The Review and Herald* (December 16, 1862).

> I am rather inclined to think that in case of a military draft, I should modify somewhat their language, and say *cannot,* instead of *will not.*[23]

It is well to compare the openness with which this subject was addressed by the pioneers to the strong, unbending position taken by the protesters in Europe in 1914. I am convinced that if these brethren had reasoned together in Christian love and understanding as was done in America during the time of the Civil War, no separation would have occurred. The work of God could have advanced unitedly and would not have been set back by many years of fighting one another.

Early in 1863 the issue of military service in the Civil War was resolved by a statement from the pen of Ellen White which can be read in *Testimonies for the Church,* vol. 1, pp. 355-368. In this testimony she warned against any fanatical actions such as those in which some of the believers in Iowa had participated. She chided those who had found fault with the suggestions of her husband and admonished the believers to remain silent about these matters. She also warned one brother who had sided with the South that unless he changed his views, he would have to be disfellowshipped from the church. Ellen White realized that a person must make a personal decision regarding his service to the government:

> *Those who feel that in the fear of God they cannot conscientiously engage in this war will be very quiet,* and when interrogated will simply state what they are obliged to say in order to answer the inquirer, and then let it be understood that they have no sympathy with the Rebellion.[24]

Ellen White put the basic question to rest by stating that,

> God's people, who are His peculiar treasure, cannot engage in this perplexing war, for it is opposed to every principle of their faith. In the army they cannot obey the truth and at the same time obey the requirements of their officers. There would be a continual violation of conscience.[25]

Then she laid down the guidelines for determining when it would be necessary to disobey the laws of the land:

> The ten precepts of Jehovah are the foundation of all righteous and good laws. Those who love God's commandments

23 J. M. Aldrich, "The War," *The Review and Herald* (December 23, 1862).

24 *Testimonies for the Church,* 1:357 (emphasis added).

25 Ibid, p. 361.

> will conform to every good law of the land. But if the requirements of the rulers are such as conflict with the laws of God, the only question to be settled is: Shall we obey God, or man?[26]

This statement seemed to stem the steady stream of discussion in the "Review and Herald" regarding the issue for a period of time. The Lord overruled the situation for His people. When the first draft law was enacted on March 3, 1863, it provided for those who did not want to obey the call. They could pay $300 and be free from that draft. Most Adventists took this route until the draft law was changed.[27]

Since this option applied to everyone, whether they had religious convictions or not, the Advent believers saw no need to make any open declaration of their beliefs relative to bearing arms. However, after this option was removed by the draft law of July 4, 1864, the Adventist leadership found it necessary to make a public declaration of their beliefs. The first of several official statements filed with State governors and the Federal Government was addressed to the Governor of Michigan. It read in part:

> The change in the law renders it necessary that we take a more public stand in the matter. For this reason we now lay before Your Excellency [Austin Blair, Governor of the state of Michigan] the sentiments of Seventh-day Adventists, as a body, relative to bearing arms, trusting that you will feel no hesitation in endorsing our claim that, as a people, we come under the intent of the late action of Congress concerning those who are conscientiously opposed to bearing arms, and are entitled to the benefits of said laws.[28]

The new law offered three provisions to exempt persons who had religious principles against participation in war: (1) guard the freed slaves, (2) work in the military hospitals, or (3) pay $300 to the government. Since $300 was a sizable sum in those days, the way was now open to save this money and serve in a capacity where there would be no conflict with conscience.

Several articles and news items appeared in the Review during this time describing the duties of hospital work and the condition of the freed slaves. As a preface to one of these, the following statement was made:

---

26 Ibid, pp. 361-62.

27 Francis M. Wilcox, *Seventh-day Adventists in Time of War* (Washington, DC: Review & Herald Publishing Assn., 1936) p. 58.

28 *The Review and Herald*, August 23, 1864; see also *SDA Encyclopedia*, "Noncombatancy" (Washington, DC: Review & Herald Publishing Assn., 1976), p. 978.

> As those who are conscientiously opposed to bearing arms can be assigned to the care of the freedmen, if they so choose, instead of paying the $300, or going to do duty in the hospitals, any information concerning these freedmen is of interest. The following sketch which we extract from an article in the American Missionary of September, shows in what condition they come into our lines, and gives something of an idea of what is to be done in taking care of them.[29]

Clearly the leadership of the church believed these alternatives to be acceptable and in accordance with the light given to them by the Lord.

Several brethren who were drafted soon after this time had difficulty in obtaining the exception as provided by the new law. Many of the military commanders did not understand how they were to handle the situation. With this problem in mind, as well as that of ministers being called to military service, Brother White made a proposal:

> [Since] the next draft will take about one in three of able-bodied men, liable to the draft. . . . We are in favor of raising a fund for the benefit of our efficient preachers who are liable to a draft. And we would set the sum for each to pay into the treasury at $100. Those faithful and true laborers who have not the $100, have friends in Christ who would gladly donate this sum for them. The interest we have in this matter for our fellow-laborers in particular is sufficient to induce us to pledge $100 to such a fund, for the benefit of those only who pay, or their friends for them, the sum of $100 each into the treasury.[30]

Please note that this proposal was specifically for workers in the cause of God and not directed toward the membership as a whole. For the membership there was also concern, but in another manner:

> If this war continues, God only knows what it will do for even non-combatants. Unless Heaven interposes, they may not always be treated with that respect and mercy they now receive.[31]

Many additional articles appeared instructing the believers how to obtain the necessary exemption from combatant service. To make the issue clearer in the minds of the people, a series of articles appeared from the

29 "Freedmen," *The Review and Herald* (September 13, 1864).
30 James White, *The Review and Herald* (January 24, 1865).
31 Ibid.

pen of R. F. Cottrell entitled, "Should the Christian Fight?" In these articles he showed that the Christian is to obey the laws of the land up to the point where such obedience would require disobeying the law of God. He warned against participation in any action of disloyalty to the government:

> If they do not, but favor opposition or rebellion, by their votes or in any other way, the church has a right to call them to an account. . . . If they persist, and will not hear the discipline of the church, she may inflict her capital punishment—the withdrawal of fellowship. If on the other hand, they go beyond the discipline—the Bible—by taking up arms in defense of civil government, the church has the same remedy, and are bound by the law of Christ, and are not justly chargeable with the crime of disloyalty.[32]

This principle was already in operation in the church before this time.

> As voluntary enlistment into the service of war is contrary to the principles of faith and practice of Seventh-day Adventists as contained in the commandments of God and the faith of Jesus, they cannot retain those within their communion who so enlist. Enoch Hayes was therefore excluded from the membership of the Battle Creek church, by a unanimous vote of the church, March 4, 1865.[33]

Clearly the church leaders took the position of noncombatancy during the Civil War, but not the position of total conscientious objection as is claimed by the Reform Movement.

Developments after the American Civil War

The Civil War ended soon after this, and the problem of military service for American Adventists did as well. However, as the work spread beyond the borders of the United States, difficulties again arose, especially in the countries of Europe. In those lands where military service was demanded of every male, even in peacetime, a new situation presented itself.

Ellen White did not seem too concerned with service in the military in peacetime draft. She wrote from Basel, Switzerland, on September 2, 1886:

> We have just said farewell to three of our responsible men in the office who were summoned by the government to serve for three weeks of drill. It was a very important stage of our work

32 R. F. Cottrell, "Should Christians Fight?" *The Review and Herald* (May 30, 1865).
33 *The Review and Herald* (March 7, 1865).

> in the publishing house, but the government calls do not accommodate themselves to our convenience. They demand that young men whom they have accepted as soldiers shall not neglect the exercise and drill essential for soldier service. We were glad to see that these men with their regimentals had tokens of honor for faithfulness in their work. They were trustworthy young men.
>
> These did not go from choice, but because the laws of their nation required this. We gave them a word of encouragement to be found true soldiers of the cross of Christ. Our prayers will follow these young men, that the angels of God may go with them and guard them from every temptation.[34]

This situation laid the foundation for later difficulties. It is a fact that Adventists in Germany were drafted into the military in peacetime and only refused service on the Sabbath, but not all military service as such.[35]

> European church leaders had made no concerted effort to acquaint their respective governments with Adventist objections to bearing arms or to performing routine labor on the Sabbath. The rapid course of events immediately preceding the outbreak of hostilities prevented their giving even members counsel on what were certain to be points of conflict with army officers. Autocratic governments like those of Germany and Russia expected implicit obedience from their subjects; their conscription laws made no provisions for noncombatant service for conscientious objectors.
>
> Failure to prepare for the problems posed by the draft became acute in Germany. There on August 4, 1914, the president of the East German Union Conference, after counseling with several associates, "informed the German War Ministry in writing . . . that conscripted Seventh-day Adventists would bear arms as combatants and would render service on the Sabbath in defense of their country." Although this was directly contrary to the position taken by Adventism's founding fathers fifty years earlier, many German church members complied with their leader's announced policy. . . .
>
> Several years after the close of the war, Adventist leaders from all over Europe met in council in Gland, Switzerland. Here

34 *Selected Messages,* book. 2, p. 335.
35 Personal account of O. Kramer's experiences in Germany at the beginning of World War I. (tape, "Rise and Progress").

> on January 2, 1923, they officially went on record as opposing all combatant service and Sabbath work other than of a humanitarian nature. This statement had the concurrence of the German leaders, who acknowledged that they had made a mistake in judgment in 1914. Although the Gland statement specified the reasons for the Seventh-day Adventist position, it also recognized that each church member possessed "absolute liberty to serve his country, at all times and in all places, in accord with the dictates of his personal conscientious conviction."[36]

The latter portion of this statement did not sit well with the members of the Reform Movement inasmuch as they do not accept the concept of individual responsibility. Reformers feel that if any freedom of conscience is given to the members, the church is not fulfilling its responsibility.

In the United States the problem of military service in World War I developed more slowly. This allowed the leadership to give greater study to these matters. On June 5, 1917, every man between the ages of 21 and 30 was required to register for the draft. The law made no provision for those who refused all forms of military service, only those who had religious beliefs opposing combatancy. Such men were permitted to perform other duties according to what the President defined as noncombatant work.

Since men were to be assigned according to their abilities, American Adventists decided that they would have the fewest Sabbath difficulties if they served in the medical corps. To provide for a more likely acceptance into this service, the church instituted training programs toward that end. In July 1918 the General Conference council held in Washington,

> decided to provide the funds for the organizing of schools for intensive training of Seventh-day Adventist young men of draft age, who have not had previous nurses' training, to prepare them to take up medical corps work when entering actual service.[37]

This is how the Adventist commitment to medical work in the military began. But the Adventist position is totally unacceptable in the eyes of Reformers. They are convinced that even wearing the military uniform is taking part in an institution designed to kill and makes the person a participant in human destruction. They are convinced that performing medical work in the military assists the war effort and the taking of life and so is a violation of the commandments of God.

---

36 *Light Bearers to the Remnant*, pp. 424-25.
37 *Seventh-day Adventists in Time of War*, p. 144.

Since the declaration of the principle of noncombatancy was made by the Adventist pioneers during the Civil War, the basic principle of action has remained the same. That principle is to cooperate with the government in every way possible until the government's commands conflict with the law of God. The leadership discourages enlistment.[38] The church clearly encourages a noncombatant position for all its members.

During the Civil War the church did not take disciplinary action on the cases of its members who had been drafted into military service, and it does not today. Never has the church, either during the Civil War or later, taken the stand (which Reformers claim was taken) to refuse noncombatant service. The church has never taken the position of total conscientious objection (refusing any military service).

There is only one real difference in the church's position between the Civil War and the present time. Instead of disfellowshipping those who enlist, the church tries to work through love to win these erring ones back to the place where the Lord would have them. It realizes—just as could be seen by the differences of opinion expressed in the pages of the "Review" during the Civil War—that people are at different stages of spiritual growth and need to be worked with rather than condemned. The church does not approve of combatant service by its members. On the other hand it realizes that it was not commissioned by the Lord to condemn, but rather to work for the salvation of sinners.

Reformers cannot be faulted for saying that they take what they consider to be a stricter position than the Adventist Church. But when they try to prove that they are taking the position of the pioneers, they are perpetrating a falsehood. They point to the mistakes made by some church leaders in Europe during World War I as proof that the church has rejected the Lord and has been rejected by Him. At the same time they do not condemn the church for the positions taken by some leaders during the Civil War. The sad fact is that most Reformers do not even know what position was taken at that time.

The Reform Movement's position is much more dogmatic, but not necessarily correct in light of the message of the Bible and Testimonies. When they accuse the church of having "fallen" because of the mistakes of leadership in Europe during World War I, let them not forget that the pioneer leaders during the American Civil War were not all clear on the issue either. Did the Lord reject the church at that time? Did Ellen White err by not condemning the brethren who did their required military drill in Switzerland after her statements in *Testimonies for the Church,* vol. 1, during the Civil War? This is a point every Reformer should consider.

38 *The Review and Herald* (June 7, 1864).

Chapter 6

Mistaken Concepts—Part 2

Liberty of Conscience

The concept of individual responsibility and freedom of conscience has caused much misunderstanding between Reformers and the Adventist Church. The Reformers insist that the church must hold up strict standards for the people to follow. In many cases the members themselves expect the church to specify every detail of how they are to act in any given situation. Little room is given for one to make decisions for himself.

The Adventist Church has given more latitude to its members by encouraging them to search the Scriptures for themselves. It has emphasized the need for every person to make moral decisions in accordance with the understanding he or she has gained from personal study of the Bible and Spirit of Prophecy. This different approach has led Reformers to believe that Adventists have lowered the standard of Christian living. Nothing could be further from the truth. The standard is given to man in God's Word. No one need doubt what is required. Let us look at what is written for us in the *Testimonies.*

> God deals with men as individuals, giving to everyone his work. All are to be taught of God. Through the grace of Christ every soul must work out his own righteousness, maintaining a living connection with the Father and the Son. This is a genuine experience that is of value.[1]

> God has appointed no man to be conscience for his fellowman. . . . For years there has been a growing tendency for men placed in positions of responsibility to lord it over God's heritage, thus removing from church members their keen sense of the need of divine instruction and an appreciation of the privilege to counsel with God regarding their duty. This order of things must be changed. There must be a reform.[2]

---

1 *Testimonies to Ministers,* p. 488.
2 Ibid., pp. 477-78.

> As a people our faith and practice need to be energized by the Holy Spirit. No ruling power that would compel man to obey the dictates of the finite mind should be exercised. "Cease ye from man, whose breath is in his nostrils," the Lord commands. By turning the minds of men to lean on human wisdom, we place a veil between God and man, so that there is not a seeing of Him who is invisible.[3]
>
> The earth was dark through misapprehension of God. That the gloomy shadows might be lightened, that the world might be brought back to God, Satan's deceptive power was to be broken. This could not be done by force. *The exercise of force is contrary to the principles of God's government; He desires only the service of love; and love cannot be commanded; it cannot be won by force or authority. Only by love is love awakened.* To know God is to love Him; His character must be manifested in contrast to the character of Satan. This work only one Being in all the universe could do. Only He who knew the height and depth of the love of God could make it known. Upon the world's dark night the Sun of Righteousness must rise, "with healing in His wings." Mal. 4:2.[4]
>
> This message is spoken to our churches in every place. In the false experience that has been coming in, a decided influence is at work to exalt human agencies, and to lead some to depend on human judgment, and to follow the control of human minds. This influence is diverting the mind from God. God forbid that any such experience should deepen and grow in our ranks as Seventh-day Adventists. Our petitions are to reach higher than erring man--to God. God does not confine Himself to one place or person. He looks down from heaven upon the children of men; He sees their perplexities, and is acquainted with the circumstances of every experience of life. He understands His own work upon the human heart, and needs not that any man should direct the workings of His Spirit.[5]

This concept of personal responsibility is foreign to most members of the Reform Movement. They have been taught to obey the dictates of the church without question. When a problem arises, instead of going to the

3 Ibid., p. 483.
4 *The Desire of Ages,* p. 22 (emphasis added).
5 *Testimonies to Ministers,* p. 484.

Source of all wisdom, they send a letter to the leaders of the General Conference. The reply from leadership is then used to stop all further discussion on the subject at hand.

When a believer realizes his ultimate accountability is to God, he will actually live up to a higher standard than any laid down by a church body. Trusting in the decisions of ecclesiastical bodies will cause much hypocrisy. People will live up to these rules only as long as they are watched. Their fear is of people, not of God.

Personal liberty and love for God combine to make a stronger congregational unity than can be achieved by arbitrary force. Note the following comment by the Spirit of Prophecy:

> When men are bound together, not by force or self-interest, but by love, they show the working of an influence that is above every human influence. Where this oneness exists, it is evident that the image of God is being restored in humanity, that a new principle of life has been implanted. It shows that there is a power in the divine nature to withstand the supernatural agencies of evil, and that the grace of God subdues the selfishness inherent in the natural heart.[6]

Divorce and Remarriage

Another concern, about which the Reform Movement refuses to accept the plain teachings of the Bible and the Spirit of Prophecy, is the matter of divorce and remarriage. Jesus said, "And I say unto you, Whosoever shall put away his wife, *except it be for fornication,* and shall marry another, committeth adultery: and whoso marrieth her which is put away doth commit adultery" (Matt 19:9).

The teaching of the Reformers is, "Whosoever shall put away his wife, *even if it be for fornication,* and shall marry another, committeth adultery." This stand is not only a perversion of the Bible but also of the clear instruction of the Spirit of Prophecy. Note the following:

> A woman may be legally divorced from her husband by the laws of the land and yet not divorced in the sight of God and according to the higher law. *There is only one sin, which is adultery, which can place the husband or wife in a position where they can be free from the marriage vow in the sight of God.* Although the laws of the land may grant a divorce, yet they are husband and wife still in the Bible light, according to the laws of God.

6 *The Desire of Ages,* p. 678.

> I saw that Sister —, as yet, has no right to marry another man; but *if she, or any other woman, should obtain a divorce legally on the ground that her husband was guilty of adultery, then she is free to be married to whom she chooses.*[7]

The stand taken by the Reform Movement on this subject is that no matter what has taken place in a marital breakup, there is no possibility for the innocent party to be restored to church membership if he or she remarries. Many injustices and inequities have arisen because of such a stand, and many souls have been driven from the church as a result.

Divorce with remarriage is looked upon as a sin which cannot be pardoned. I personally know many persons who were disfellowshipped because of a divorce/remarriage situation. They attended church faithfully for years, paid their tithes regularly, and were obedient to the rules of the church in other matters. Yet they could not be restored to membership, even though they may have been innocent parties.

The servant of God did not take this stand. Many other statements could be presented to show how Ellen White endorsed the right of the innocent party to remarry. The leaders of the Reform are not ignorant of these statements; they simply refuse to accept them. Time and again this has been discussed in delegates' sessions of the Reform General Conference (IMS).

The rationale for refusing these statements has always been: If we accept this, we will be no better than the Adventist Church. Sometimes the issue is covered by the excuse that such a policy would be too difficult to administer. As a delegate to the 1978 delegate session, I also rationalized that, "It is too difficult to determine who is really innocent." While this may be true, it is only an excuse for the church's not accepting what is written; instead, "they [teach] for doctrines the commandments of men."

Many Reformers continue to take a very negative view of the marriage relationship. In the past some leaders taught that husbands and wives were to live as "brother and sister." This view, although no longer openly taught, still influences the lives of some of the leaders and members.

Without question, the marriage relationship is under attack in this present evil world. Divorce was never in God's plan. On the other hand we will not achieve the gospel commission by taking an extreme view of the issue. Our only safety is in searching the Word of God and then teaching the believers to bring their lives into accordance with its principles. Let us not forget that the purpose of the church is not to condemn, but to save.

The stand presently taken in the Reform Movement can be likened to

7 Ellen G. White, *The Adventist Home* (Nashville: Southern Publishing Assoc., 1952), p. 344 (emphasis added).

that of the church leaders in the time of Christ. "And the scribes and Pharisees brought unto him a woman taken in adultery; and when they had set her in the midst, They say unto him, Master, this woman was taken in adultery, in the very act. Now Moses in the law commanded us, that such should be stoned: but what sayest thou?" (John 8:3-5).

I fear that many Reformers would not have welcomed the Saviour's words. They might have rejected Him as the Son of God because of them. After all, He did not seem to be upholding the law. "When Jesus had lifted up himself, and saw none but the woman, he said unto her, Woman, where are those thine accusers? hath no man condemned thee? She said, No man, Lord. And Jesus said unto her, Neither do I condemn thee: go, and sin no more" (John 8:10-11). She was never punished for her wrongdoing.

I am thankful for the words of Jesus! No person is so deep in sin that he cannot obtain pardon at the foot of the cross. There is hope for each of us. Praise God for this truth! How wonderful it would be if each of us would think about the admonition of Christ: "He that is without sin among you, let him first cast a stone at her" (John 8:7).

Healthful Living

The message of healthful living is one of the great truths given to the Advent people. The Lord gave this message to prepare a people to stand in the last great crisis. According to the Spirit of Prophecy the doctrine of health is to the church what the right arm is to the body. No one can question the benefits to be achieved by following the directions given by the Spirit of Prophecy on this subject. Properly understood and lived, they can bring health and an increased life span, as medical research has proven.

When the message becomes perverted, however, it can result in fanaticism, illness, or death. The Reform Movement has stressed the health message, but often without proper direction or true understanding. In essence, their entire health message centers around diet. Very little is ever mentioned about exercise and the need for sufficient rest.

People in those areas of the world who take the most extreme positions on diet know little or nothing about simple sanitation. For example, I think of an experience I had while visiting one of the countries of Central America. The mission operated a bakery on its grounds. Supposedly, the workers prepared good healthful bread. To my shock, the rising loaves were covered with flies. A cat ran freely through the bakery, and a parrot sat in an open window nearby. The director saw no problem with these conditions, even though he was overly strict in other areas of healthful living.

True health reform deals with all areas of life, not just one. Where are the programs conducted by the Reform Movement to help people obtain victory over the tobacco habit, for example, or programs to help people begin a new, more healthful lifestyle? The Reform (IMS) has only one institution in Germany and a few treatment rooms in some countries which even attempt to do such work.

The Spirit of Prophecy appeals to the people to live up to the light the Lord has given in regard to healthful living. If they neglect or disregard the message, they will suffer the results, not only physically but spiritually as well. Yet the church has not been authorized to force its members into submission to its dietary ideals. I will quote only one of many statements on this subject, especially addressed to the matter of flesh foods.

> We do not mark out any precise line to be followed in diet; but we do say that in countries where there are fruits, grains, and nuts in abundance, flesh food is not the right food for God's people. I have been instructed that flesh food has a tendency to animalize the nature, to rob men and women of that love and sympathy which they should feel for everyone, and to give the lower passions control over the higher powers of the being. If meat eating was ever healthful, it is not safe now. Cancers, tumors, and pulmonary diseases are largely caused by meat eating.[8]

On the basis of the above and similar statements, the Reform Movement has made it a worldwide test of fellowship that no flesh may be eaten by its members. This stand, though well meant, bars the proclamation of the last message from countries where other foods than flesh are not readily available. How would it be possible for the Reformers to bring the message to the Eskimos, for example? Despite the fact that I am a confirmed vegetarian, I see that this unbending stand limits the outreach of the gospel. In addition it places the teachings of the church above that of the Bible and the Spirit of Prophecy.

At a seminar I taught in Central America some of the students asked me to confirm their conviction that Christ, while on earth, did not eat fish. Rather than answer their question with a yes or no, I suggested that we turn to the Scriptures. The Bible plainly stated that Christ ate fish along with the disciples. Even after His resurrection He ate fish. "And they gave him a piece of a broiled fish, and of an honeycomb. And he took it, and did eat before them" (Luke 24:42-43). This so shocked the students that I feared they would lose their faith in Christ. Health reform had become so distorted in their minds that it took precedence over the example of Jesus.

---

8 *Testimonies for the Church,* 9:159.

Neither the Bible nor the Spirit of Prophecy promotes such distortions of the real message for these last days. Immediately following the previously quoted statement, we find the following:

> *We are not to make the use of flesh food a test of fellowship,* but we should consider the influence that professed believers who use flesh foods have over others. As God's messengers, shall we not say to the people: "Whether therefore ye eat, or drink, or whatsoever ye do, do all to the glory of God"? I Corinthians 10:31. Shall we not bear a decided testimony against the indulgence of perverted appetite? Will any who are ministers of the gospel, proclaiming the most solemn truth ever given to mortals, set an example in returning to the fleshpots of Egypt?[9]

There is a great difference between bearing a decided testimony and enforcing a test of fellowship. There is a great difference between commanding people in the way they should go and what is directed in the gospel commission. "Go ye therefore, and teach all nations, baptizing them in the name of the Father, and of the Son, and of the Holy Ghost: Teaching them to observe all things whatsoever I have commanded you: and, lo, I am with you alway, even unto the end of the world" (Matt 28:19-20). There is no commission to force converts into following the dictates of the church.

This matter was discussed in a committee of the Reform Movement (IMS). It was declared that although the Spirit of Prophecy prohibited making the use of flesh food a test of fellowship, the General Conference had the authority to make its use a test. Such a position is an insult to the principle that all doctrines must be based on a plain "Thus saith the Lord."

By making the matter of meat eating a test of fellowship, the Reformers are in direct violation of the writings of the servant of the Lord. Their action virtually bars the kingdom from those who may not be able, because of circumstances, to live out this part of the message fully. Thus the message of healthful living has turned into a curse rather than a blessing.

In many areas of the world the Reformers have perverted the health message by giving it precedence over the three angels' messages, and even the Ten Commandments. In those areas the health message has changed from the right arm to being the entire body. This the Lord never intended.

I urge each to study the light given and to bring his or her life into conformity to that light. Do not look at others. You will not have to answer for them. We will have to answer for ourselves to the Lord for the use we have made of the light given. Let us realize our personal responsibility.

---

9 Ibid., pp. 159-60 (emphasis added).

Chapter 7
Divergent Doctrines

Since the Seventh-day Adventist Reform Movement claims to be the true Advent movement, it is important to understand in what areas their teachings diverge from commonly held Adventist doctrines. We have touched already on some of these. In this section we will explore additional points of difference.

The 1888 Message

Reformers firmly believe that God called their movement into existence and that it was prophesied to come. They must, therefore, provide evidence for this position. Two events are cited.

First, they assert that since the Adventist leadership "overthrew the commandments of God in 1914," they have a right to exist as a separate movement. However, there is some realization that just this one event is very weak ground for establishing a new movement in opposition to the church raised up by God in the great Advent awakening. Secondly, Reformers look for additional justification in the events of 1888. Here, they affirm, are the real beginnings of the movement.

In the Reformation Study Course they cite from the *Testimonies* negative statements regarding the condition of the church, both previous to that conference and afterward. They uplift the message brought by the brethren Jones and Waggoner as a special message from God, as it truly was. The Reformers insist that the church rejected this message.

Ellen G. White referred to this message about righteousness by faith as being the beginning of the loud cry:

> The time of test is just upon us, for the loud cry of the third angel has already begun in the revelation of the righteousness of Christ, the sin-pardoning Redeemer. This is the beginning of the light of the angel whose glory shall fill the whole earth.[1]

---

1 *The Review and Herald* (November 22, 1892), quoted in A. G. Daniells, *Christ Our Righteousness* (Washington, DC: Review & Herald Publishing Assn., 1941), p. 56.

Since some of the church leaders opposed this message and the messengers in 1888, Reformers reason, the Lord had to give the message to others so that it could be proclaimed in clarity. They look upon themselves as the ones called to fulfill this task. In lesson 16 of the Reformation Study Course, they theorize that the message to come out from Babylon now includes calling people from the "fallen Adventist Church."

For comparison, I will quote their reasoning and then the light given to us in the pages of the Spirit of Prophecy. First, the Reformers state:

> The second angel in 1844 proclaimed the fall of all the existing churches. He stated that they had become Babylon, which means confusion. This message will be proclaimed continually until the end of time. Yet the angel of Revelation 18 repeats the same message. We ask, Why is this necessary? The answer is, Because something that had not yet fallen in 1844 is now declared fallen. The community which is called Babylon in the second angel's message is apparently increased or enlarged. *It is not simply that their fall had not yet reached its peak*, but mainly that some bodies of Christians that were not included in the message of denunciation by the second angel in 1844 are now included in this company by strength of the message of the other angel.[2]

Compare the above statement now with the insight from the Spirit of Prophecy:

> The second angel's message of Revelation 14 was first preached in the summer of 1844, and it then had a more direct application to the churches of the United States, where the warning of the judgment had been most widely proclaimed and most generally rejected, and where the declension in the churches had been most rapid. *But the message of the second angel did not reach its complete fulfillment in 1844. The churches then experienced a moral fall, in consequence of their refusal of the light of the advent message; but that fall was not complete.* As they have continued to reject the special truths for this time they have fallen lower and lower. Not yet, however, can it be said that "Babylon is fallen, . . . because she made *all nations* drink of the wine of the wrath of her fornication." She has not yet made all nations do this. The spirit of world conforming and indifference

2 *Reformation Study Course*, Lesson 16, International Missionary Society, S.D.A. Reform Movement (emphasis added).

> to the testing truths for our time exists and has been gaining ground in churches of the Protestant faith in all the countries of Christendom; and these churches are included in the solemn and terrible denunciation of the second angel. *But the work of apostasy has not yet reached its culmination.*
>
> As these bodies depart further and further from the truth, and ally themselves more closely with the world, the difference between the two classes will widen, and it will finally result in separation.[3]

It is clear that Ellen White refers to the fallen churches as reaching a further stage of apostasy that necessitates the second call to go forth. She is not in any way applying the call of Revelation 18 to a call to come out of the Seventh-day Adventist Church. Another statement underscores this.

In the *Review and Herald,* October 17, 1893—please note that this was after the conference of 1888—Ellen White makes the following statement:

> How is it that these pamphlets denouncing the Seventh-day Adventist Church as Babylon were scattered abroad everywhere, at the very time when that church was receiving the outpouring of the Spirit of God? *How is it that men can be so deceived as to imagine that the loud cry consists in calling the people of God out from the fellowship of a church that is enjoying a season of refreshing?* Oh, may these deceived souls come into the current, and receive the blessing, and be endued with power from on high.[4]

> Those who receive the *Testimonies* as the message of God will be helped and blessed thereby; but those who take them in parts, simply to support some theory or idea of their own, to vindicate themselves in a course of error, will not be blessed and benefited by what they teach. To claim that the Seventh-day Adventist Church is Babylon, is to make the same claim as does Satan, who is an accuser of the brethren, who accuses them before God night and day.[5]

It is strange that the Reformers seem to know that the Lord rejected the Adventist Church because of the events at the Minneapolis Conference in 1888. Yet the prophet of the Lord did not seem to know of any such rejection! She wrote in December of 1892:

3 *The Great Controversy,* pp. 389-90 (emphasis added).
4 *Testimonies to Ministers,* p. 23 (emphasis added).
5 Ibid., p. 42.

> In reviewing our past history, having traveled over every step of advance to our present standing, I can say, Praise God! As I see what God has wrought, I am filled with astonishment and with confidence in Christ as Leader. We have nothing to fear for the future, except as we shall forget the way the Lord has led us, and His teaching in our past history. We are now a strong people, if we will put our trust in the Lord; for we are handling the mighty truths of the word of God. We have everything to be thankful for.[6]

Reformers go astray in discussing the matters of 1888. In general they do not understand what was the central issue at this momentous conference. They draw a blanket assumption that the entire church rejected the message. But this does not match the facts.

First of all, no position was ever voted by the delegates at the conference. It was not even a voting matter. The messages were presented at the ministerial institute rather than at the General Conference delegate session.

Secondly, while no one can deny that some of the leading brethren did reject the message, many others rejoiced in the light given. Rather than being suppressed in the ensuing years, the message was strongly promoted by the brethren Jones and Waggoner with the cooperation of Ellen White. The message of righteousness by faith was presented at one camp meeting and one ministerial institute after another until its glory permeated the church.

After a period of time many of those leading brethren who had rejected the message repented. In 1893 Elder George I. Butler, who had been the President of the General Conference up to 1888 and was very strongly opposed to the presentation of the message, repented and placed himself fully on the side of truth and asked forgiveness for his previous actions.[7]

Another opponent to the message in 1888 was Elder Uriah Smith. Ellen White rejoiced when she was able to write on January 12, 1891:

> I learn that on Sabbath Elder Smith made quite full confessions and Brother Rubert also confessed. They went back in their confessions to the meeting at Minneapolis, and confessed their mistakes, in their blindness, and that their spirit and actions on that occasion were wrong. The Lord had precious truth unfold to His people which they, being filled with unbelief and

6 *Selected Messages,* book. 3, p. 162.

7 A. V. Olson, *Thirteen Crisis Years,* 1888-1901 (Washington, DC: Review & Herald Publishing Assn., 1891) pp. 92-93.

> prejudice, could not appreciate, and they worked counter to the Spirit of God.[8]

Rather than take the limited space to quote additional documentation for the correction in course taken by the leaders of the Adventist Church after 1888, I urge the reader to study the book by A. V. Olson, which I mentioned earlier, *Thirteen Crisis Years* (previously published under the title *Through Crisis to Victory*).

In conclusion we must ask another question. The Reformers claim that the Adventist Church rejected the message of Justification by Faith in 1888 and thus prepared themselves to be overthrown by the Lord. We ask: Have the Reformers ever fully accepted this message, and are they proclaiming it to the world? This can be answered with an emphatic NO!

Some Reformers in recent years have begun to proclaim this message. But as one views the situation on the worldwide scene, he sees an entirely different picture. When I became division president and began traveling in Central America, I found ignorance in regard to this most important truth. In every location the Reform Movement was steeped in total legalism. When the message of justification by faith was presented, it came as a totally unheard-of doctrine, and the Reform leaders in these countries opposed it.

I call upon Reformers to acknowledge that while they have been accusing the Advent people of rejecting an important message, they have been the ones who actually have rejected it. With all due respect to those who have been misled by others, they must realize that Reform leadership has taken the position of the "accuser of the brethren."

I appeal to the members in the Reform Movements to study the facts. You will see how your leaders have constructed a false history in order to justify themselves and "to draw away disciples after them." I urge you to study in detail the message which was presented by the brethren in 1888 and your hearts will be warmed. You will experience a deeper love for the Lord and will begin to enjoy your Christian experience as never before.

The 144,000

Another area where Reformers take a divergent doctrinal view is the subject of the 144,000. Whereas in the Adventist Church this matter has become almost a nonissue, to Reformers the topic is very important. They hold to the view (expressed by Elder J. N. Loughborough) that the number 144,000 is a literal rather than a symbolic number, and that it includes

8 Manuscript 40, 1891 (quoted in *Thirteen Crisis Years*, pp. 102-3).

all those who have died under the three angels' messages. In trying to prove this point they quote several statements from some of the Adventist pioneers as well as some early statements by Ellen White. They especially cherish a statement from her first vision: "The living saints, 144,000 in number, knew and understood the voice."[9]

To them this statement is definitive. However, it seems that the closer to the end of her life the prophet came, the more uncertain she seemed to be in regard to who composed this special group. In every other statement she just refers to this number as a special class without specifying whether it is to be considered a literal number or only symbolic of that special group of people who will be living and prepared to meet the Lord when He comes.

In 1901 she made the following significant statement:

> Christ says that there will be those in the church who will present fables and suppositions, when God has given grand, elevating, ennobling truths which should ever be kept in the treasure house of the mind. When men pick up this theory and that theory, when they are curious to know something it is not necessary for them to know, God is not leading them. It is not His plan that His people shall present something which they have to suppose, which is not taught in the Word. It is not His will that they shall get into controversy over questions which will not help them spiritually, such as, Who is to compose the hundred and forty-four thousand? This those who are the elect of God will in a short time know without question.[10]

The Reformation Study Course rationalizes that although we are not to get into controversy over who this group is, we can be certain that this is the sum total of all the redeemed under the threefold angels' message. Thus the authors of the Study Course totally disregard the above statement. This shows the fallacy in trying to rationalize our positions or in adding to what the Word of God reveals. We need to accept what the Lord has seen fit to open to the understanding of His people and be willing to yield to the fact that there are some matters which are not clearly revealed.

Let me summarize, now, the Reform teaching on the 144,000:

1. Only 144,000 persons will be redeemed through the preaching of the three angels' messages in the period extending from 1844 to the end of time.

2. Most of these redeemed persons, however, are presently in the

9 *Early Writings,* p. 15.
10 *Selected Messages,* book 1, p. 174.

churches of Babylon and will come out during the latter rain.

The larger question is, How does this teaching affect the spiritual growth of the Reform Movement? The answer quickly becomes evident. If one believes the above, there will be little zeal for active evangelism. Members can sit back in complacency and say, Soon the Lord will pour out His spirit upon us, and the work will be finished quickly.

This doctrine excuses the small numbers and explains away the many defects in the Movement. Reformers reason, After all, very few will be saved; so if you only stay with the Reform ship, all will turn out right. In the main Reformers lack an understanding of the gospel commission and the place of the church of God in this work.

Closed Communion

Another teaching and practice which sets the Reform Movement apart from Adventist thinking is its position on the observance of Communion. Reformers hold that since Christ held the Last Supper alone with His disciples, the Communion service is reserved only for church members who are in good standing. The Adventist practice of open Communion provides for them another "proof" that the church is a "fallen organization." In addition they take issue with the Adventist Church usage of individual cups in the Communion service. They base their stand on the biblical report that Jesus "took the cup [singular], and when he had given thanks, He gave it to them: and they all drank of it" (Mark 14:23).

Due to their high regard for their own church body, they consider the Communion service to be just as much a communion with one another as with the Lord. To omit the use of one cup means to fail to have communion with one's brothers and sisters.

Reformers use very intricate reasoning to prove that only church members may take part. Even visiting Adventists are not permitted to participate in the distribution of the bread and wine since they do not, in the eyes of Reformers, really belong to the family of God. In taking this position they neglect the clear injunction of the Spirit of Prophecy which they claim to hold so dear.

> Christ's example forbids exclusiveness at the Lord's Supper. It is true that open sin excludes the guilty. This the Holy Spirit plainly teaches. I Cor. 5:11. But beyond this none are to pass judgment. God has not left it with men to say who shall present themselves on these occasions. For who can read the heart? . . . "Let a man examine himself, and so let him eat of that bread, and drink of that cup." For "whosoever shall eat this bread, and

> drink of this cup of the Lord, unworthily, shall be guilty of the body and blood of the Lord." "He that eateth and drinketh unworthily, eateth and drinketh damnation to himself, not discerning the Lord's body." I Cor. 11:28, 27, 29.[11]

In the book *Evangelism*, pp. 276-77, Ellen White recounts an experience where a minister of another church attended an Adventist Church one Sabbath when the Communion service was held. He was invited to take part in the Communion even though he did not desire to participate in the foot washing. The servant of the Lord clearly approved of this. The Lord gave further instruction through His servant:

> There may come in among you those who are not in heart united with truth and holiness, but who may wish to take part in these services. Forbid them not.[12]

Gospel Commission

As part of His last message to the disciples, Jesus gave them their commission recorded in Matthew 28:19-20: "Go ye therefore, and teach all nations, baptizing them in the name of the Father, and of the Son, and of the Holy Ghost: Teaching them to observe all things whatsoever I have commanded you: and, lo, I am with you alway, even unto the end of the world. Amen."

We note that the commission was to teach, baptize, and teach some more in order that the believers might learn to observe all that the Lord desired them to know. There is no command for the church to enforce its dogmas upon the people on pain of excommunication if they do not follow them to the letter.

Reformers on the other hand believe the only way to show contempt for sin is to disfellowship members for any wrong action (apart from minor infractions). Since the Adventist leadership did not disfellowship Elder Conradi and his coworkers as punishment for their mistakes in World War I, they argue that the General Conference became guilty of committing the sin itself. They take this position on the basis of their understanding of several statements in the Spirit of Prophecy such as the following:

> He would teach His people that disobedience and sin are exceedingly offensive to Him and are not to be lightly regarded. He shows us that when His people are found in sin they should

11 *The Desire of Ages*, p. 656.

12 Ellen G. White, *Evangelism* (Washington, DC: Review & Herald Publishing Assn., 1946 [reprinted 1970]), p. 277.

> at once take decided measures to put that sin from them, that His frown may not rest upon them all. But if the sins of the people are passed over by those in responsible positions, His frown will be upon them, and the people of God, as a body, will be held responsible for these sins. . . . When the people realize that darkness is settling upon them, and they do not know the cause, they should seek God earnestly, in great humility and self-abasement, until the *wrongs which grieve His Spirit* are searched out and put away.[13]

We must note that the wrongs are to be put away, not the sinner. Sad to say, our human nature prompts us to hate the sinner and love the sin. We should rather love the sinner despite our hatred for the sin. There is no question that continued, open transgression against the commandments of God cannot be tolerated by the church. At the same time, we must never forget that our primary goal is to assist the sinner to find a new experience with the Lord rather than to punish him for the black name he may have given the church. Jesus gave clear instructions as to how the church was to deal with erring members in Matthew 18:11-17.

> For the Son of man is come to save that which was lost. How think ye? if a man have an hundred sheep, and one of them be gone astray, doth he not leave the ninety and nine, and goeth into the mountains, and seeketh that which is gone astray? And if so be that he find it, verily I say unto you, he rejoiceth more of that sheep, than of the ninety and nine which went not astray. Even so it is not the will of your Father which is in heaven, that one of these little ones should perish. Moreover if thy brother shall trespass against thee, go and tell him his fault between thee and him alone: if he shall hear thee, thou hast gained thy brother. But if he will not hear thee, then take with thee one or two more, that in the mouth of two or three witnesses every word may be established. And if he shall neglect to hear them, tell it unto the church: but if he neglect to hear the church, let him be unto thee as an heathen man and a publican.

We then come to the verse which has so often been abused by the Roman Church, "Verily I say unto you, Whatsoever ye shall bind on earth shall be bound in heaven: and whatsoever ye shall loose on earth shall be loosed in heaven" (vs. 18). The Roman Church understood this to mean that the church has a free hand in dealing with human souls, and that

13 *Testimonies for the Church,* 3:265 (emphasis added).

heaven will agree with every decision thus made. They do not realize that every decision made by the church should be made in view of how heaven would act in the situation.

Unfortunately Reformers take the Roman view of this matter. But note: only *after* every possible step is taken to effect restoration, is the church to dismiss a member from fellowship. This should be done with the understanding that even then the objective of such an action is to awaken the sinner to his need and hopefully to bring about his restoration. How are we to treat "an heathen man and a publican"? We should try to win him to Christ. In the same chapter, Peter is admonished by Jesus Himself to be willing to forgive a brother as often as he repents (Matt 18:22).

Such longsuffering action is not in agreement with the underlying spirit of the Reformers. They believe that in order to rid the church of sin they must remove every "sinner." When this kind of procedure is followed, then the church is properly discharging its duty. Instead of working on the problem with the view of saving the sinner, Reformers commonly "solve" the problem by removing the sinner from fellowship. All too often there is a veiled, or not so veiled, threat that unless you get your life in order, the church will have to deal with you. How differently Christ works:

> The Eastern shepherd does not drive his sheep. He depends not upon force or fear; but going before, he calls them. They know his voice, and obey the call. So does the Saviour-Shepherd with His sheep. . . . It is not the fear of punishment, or the hope of everlasting reward, that leads the disciples of Christ to follow Him. They behold the Saviour's matchless love, revealed throughout His pilgrimage on earth, from the manger of Bethlehem to Calvary's cross, and the sight of Him attracts, it softens and subdues the soul. Love awakens in the heart of the beholders. They hear His voice, and they follow Him.[14]

This approach of leadership toward sinners in the congregation fosters the idea that salvation comes only through the Reform Movement. Furthermore, it is church leadership that decides who is permitted to remain members and who is not. Accordingly, leadership holds a terrible controlling power over the consciences of the people.

One General Conference leader, cautioning workers against acting too quickly in disfellowshipping people, said, "Remember that in reality when a person is disfellowshipped from the church you are pronouncing the death penalty against him." This is the same kind of autocratic power that

14 *The Desire of Ages,* p. 480.

Rome holds over its people. Members of the Reform Movement believe that to be cut off from church fellowship is to be cut off from the Lord.

The Remnant and the Laodicean Message

Since the Reform Movement regards itself as God's true people, the true remnant of Revelation 12:17, some leaders have developed a fanciful interpretation for this passage. It is taught that there are three entities in this verse: the woman, the seed, and the remnant. The woman is identified as the Protestant churches. "Her seed" is said to represent the Adventist Church; the "remnant" is taken to refer to the Reform Movement. Thus, the attempt is made to justify it as a separate organization.

However, to split the phrase, "the remnant of her seed," and argue that it symbolizes two separate organizations, is to distort the passage. The next clause ("*which* keeps the commandments . . . and have the testimony") clearly demonstrates that the expression ("the remnant of her seed") is referring to a *single* entity which has two major characteristics.

Similarly, the Reformers argue that the warnings given to the Laodicean church are addressed to the Adventist General Conference leadership and indicate God's rejection of the Adventist Church. In an attempt to find a biblical foundation for this view, they note that the message is addressed "to the angel of the church," which they assume is the church's leadership.

In order to understand this message properly and to see to whom it is addressed, several things need to be taken into consideration:

1. Not every "church" addressed in these messages was a single organized body. For example, the church of Sardis must be understood as a composite of all the various Protestant denominations. The message was directed toward every believer in Christ who lived in this church period.

2. The very same could be said for the church of Philadelphia under which symbol the times of the "Great Advent Awakening" are depicted. Here again the message applied to believers from every Protestant denomination who held only one thing in common: the soon coming of Christ.

3. Likewise the Laodicean message applies to the last time period of church history and to every believer in Christ living in this time regardless of denominational affiliation.

Let us carefully note how Ellen White made some specific applications of the Laodicean message.

Ellen White applied the Laodicean message to God's people even before the Adventist Church was organized or named:

> In the spring of 1857, . . . The testimony to the Laodicean church was generally received; but some in the East were

> making bad use of it. Instead of applying it to their own hearts, so as to be benefited by it themselves, they were using the testimony to oppress others.[15]

Please note three important things regarding this statement:

1. The name Seventh-day Adventist was not adopted until 1860, three years after Ellen White applied the message to the people of God.

2. The General Conference was not organized until 1863, six years after this message was applied by Ellen White to God's people. Thus the Laodicean message did not single out the leadership of the General Conference as the Reformers claim that it does.

3. The message is to be applied to each of us personally in order for it to do its work. It is not to be used to point a finger at others.

> I have seen that it was not the design of the message to lead brother to sit in judgment over his brother, to tell him what to do, and just how far to go; but for each individual to search his own heart, and attend to his own individual work.[16]

The letter to the Laodicean church, therefore, bears on it, as it were, our individual names. Remember that there are two classes of Laodiceans: those who stay in their deplorable condition, and those who heed the counsel of the True Witness. To attempt to use the Laodicean message in such a way as to "prove" the rejection of the Adventist Church is to misuse the Scriptures. Such attempts were already being made in the days of Ellen White and are addressed in the following statement:

> They would tear down that which God would restore by the Laodicean message. He wounds only that He may heal, not cause to perish. The Lord lays upon no man a message that will discourage and dishearten the church. *He reproves, He rebukes, He chastens; but it is only that He may restore and approve at last.*[17]

The cure for Laodiceanism is for each believer to realize his or her personal spiritual condition and to accept from the Lord the necessary medicine. The medicine is the realization that all our righteousness is unacceptable by the Lord and that our only hope is in receiving His righteousness in its place. Note the following Spirit of Prophecy insight:

---

15 Ellen G. White, *Spiritual Gifts* 2 (Washington, DC: Review and Herald, 1945 [first published in Battle Creek, 1858]): 222-23.

16 Ibid., p. 223.

17 *Testimonies to Ministers*, p. 23 (emphasis added).

> The Laodicean message has been sounding. Take this message in all its phases and sound it forth to the people wherever Providence opens the way. Justification by faith and the righteousness of Christ are the themes to be presented to a perishing world.[18]

Self-glorification and legalism run directly counter to the message of justification by faith. As we have noted, it is the Reform Movement which has rejected the message of justification by faith. By adding rule to rule for their people to follow, the Reformers have slipped into formalism and legalism. Rather than pointing the finger at Adventists, they need to realize that they are also a part of the time period of Laodicea and must apply the message to themselves as well.

Nature of the Godhead

The Reform Movement has never had a clear understanding of the nature of the Godhead. In the booklet, *Principles of Faith,* it is still stated that the Holy Spirit is a power. No mention is made that He is also a personal Being. It was not until the General Conference (IMS) session in 1978 that it was acknowledged for the first time that the Holy Spirit is actually a Person. Despite the decision to this effect, there are still leading men who strongly dispute this teaching.

Even more sad is the belief and teaching of some of the General Conference leaders regarding the divinity of Christ. Until recently, Arianism, the teaching that Christ is a created being, was taught at the mission school for potential workers. As late as the General Conference Committee (IMS) session of 1980, workers were requested to teach that Christ, while on earth, was totally human without any divinity.

When some of the workers resisted this demand with many clear statements from the Spirit of Prophecy as well as the Bible, the issue was dropped. However, a few months later an article appeared in the official organ of the General Conference (IMS), *Der Sabbatwachter and Herold der Reformation,* which presented this same teaching.

With many who hold these ideas, it seems to make no difference how much evidence there is to the contrary. Their minds cannot be changed. Always the defense is, The pioneers believed it this way, so it must be the truth. Unfortunately, it appears that many of the Reform leaders are following in the footsteps of the Jews of old. "But in vain they do worship me, teaching for doctrines the commandments of men" (Matt 15:9).

---

18 Ellen G. White Comments, *The SDA Bible Commentary* 7 (Washington, DC: Review & Herald Publishing Assn., 1957): 964.

Let us take a brief look at what the Bible and the Spirit of Prophecy teach on this issue. Jesus while on earth claimed oneness with God the Father: "I and my Father are one" (John 10:30). Likewise, the prologue to the Gospel of John asserts His eternal deity.

> In the beginning was the Word, and the Word was with God, and the Word was God. The same was in the beginning with God. All things were made by him; and without him was not anything made that was made. In him was life; and the life was the light of men. . . . And the Word was made flesh, and dwelt among us, (and we beheld his glory, as of the only begotten of the Father,) full of grace and truth (John 1:1-4, 14).

No aspect of the divinity of Christ causes more confusion than does the resurrection.

The leading brethren in the Reform Movement teach that since the angel who came to Christ's tomb stated, "Thy Father calls Thee" (*The Desire of Ages,* p. 785), it must be true that the Father raised the Son. When we continue reading in *The Desire of Ages,* however, a different picture is given.

> When the voice of the mighty angel was heard at Christ's tomb, saying, Thy Father calls Thee, *the Saviour came forth from the grave by the life that was in Himself.* Now was proved the truth of His words, "I lay down My life, that I might take it again. . . . I have power to lay it down, and I have power to take it again." Now was fulfilled the prophecy He had spoken to the priests and rulers, "Destroy this temple, and in three days I will raise it up." John 10:17, 18; 2:19.
>
> Over the rent sepulcher of Joseph Christ had proclaimed in triumph, "I am the Resurrection, and the life." *These words could be spoken only by the Deity.* All created beings live by the will and power of God. They are dependent recipients of the life of God. From the highest seraph to the humblest animate being, all are replenished from the Source of life. Only He who is one with God could say, I have power to lay down My life, and I have power to take it again. *In His divinity, Christ possessed the power to break the bonds of death.*[19]

The Spirit of Prophecy states again and again that during His life on earth, "divinity flashed through humanity." Additionally, we read,

---

19 *The Desire of Ages,* p. 785 (emphasis added).

> In Christ is life, original, unborrowed, underived. "He that hath the Son hath life." I John 5:12. The divinity of Christ is the believer's assurance of eternal life.[20]

With all the evidence regarding the divinity of Christ, why do the Reform leaders find it so difficult to accept this truth? Why do they deny His equality with the Father? Much has to do with the cultural upbringing of most of the Reform leaders.

The German child is taught from his early years to recognize a line of authority issuing from one person at the top. All below are expected to render perfect obedience to that one person. It is easy, therefore, to reason that heaven also has such a line of authority. God the Father is at the highest position. Christ is below Him in authority, and the Holy Spirit is below Jesus. For some it is incomprehensible to believe that all three work together as a unit. But to accept the teachings of the highest leaders in the Reform Movement regarding the nature of the Godhead would make it necessary to reject the words of the Bible as well as the witness of the Spirit of Prophecy.

This kind of thinking carries over into the functions of church administration too. For example, since it is thought that elected officers stand above the committee, very little thought is given to the actions of committees.

20 Ibid., p. 530.

Chapter 8

The Wheat and Tares

> Another parable put he forth unto them, saying, The kingdom of heaven is likened unto a man which sowed good seed in his field: But while men slept, his enemy came and sowed tares among the wheat, and went his way. But when the blade was sprung up, and brought forth fruit, then appeared the tares also. So the servants of the householder came and said unto him, Sir, didst not thou sow good seed in thy field? from whence then hath it tares? He said unto them, An enemy hath done this. The servants said unto him, Wilt thou then that we go and gather them up? But he said, Nay; lest while ye gather up the tares, ye root up also the wheat with them. Let both grow together until the harvest: and in the time of the harvest I will say to the reapers, gather ye together first the tares, and bind them in bundles to burn them: but gather the wheat into my barn (Matt 13:24-30).

A proper understanding of this parable is very important in the present stage of the history of the world and the church. We must not use this parable to excuse sin in our lives; neither are we to try to perform the work assigned to the angels in separating the wheat from the tares.

We have been given much instruction in the Spirit of Prophecy to assist our understanding of this significant parable. Let us study some of these statements and discover how they apply to the church today.

> In the East, men sometimes took revenge upon an enemy by strewing his newly sown fields with the seeds of some noxious weed that, while growing, closely resembled wheat. Springing up with the wheat, it injured the crop and brought trouble and loss to the owner of the field. So it is from enmity to Christ that Satan scatters his evil seed among the good grain of the kingdom. The fruit of his sowing he attributes to the Son of God. By bringing into the church those who bear Christ's name while they deny His character, the wicked one causes that God shall

> be dishonored, the work of salvation misrepresented, and souls imperiled.
>
> Christ's servants are grieved as they see true and false believers mingled in the church. They long to do something to cleanse the church. Like the servants of the householder, they are ready to uproot the tares. But Christ says to them, "Nay; lest while ye gather up the tares, ye root up also the wheat with them. Let both grow together until the harvest."
>
> Christ has plainly taught that those who persist in open sin must be separated from the church, but He has not committed to us the work of judging character and motive. He knows our nature too well to entrust this work to us. Should we try to uproot from the church those whom we suppose to be spurious Christians, we should be sure to make mistakes. Often we regard as hopeless subjects the very ones whom Christ is drawing to Himself. Were we to deal with these souls according to our imperfect judgment, it would perhaps extinguish their last hope. Many who think themselves Christians will at last be found wanting. Many will be in heaven who their neighbors supposed would never enter there. Man judges from appearance, but God judges the heart. The tares and the wheat are to grow together until the harvest; *and the harvest is the end of probationary time.*[1]

Often souls who are thought to be erring are dealt with harshly because the other members want to go on record that their actions are not acceptable. They want the church to *appear* pure. Is this a proper motive?

> The world has no right to doubt the truth of Christianity because there are unworthy members in the church, nor should Christians become disheartened because of these false brethren. How was it with the early church? Ananias and Saphira joined themselves to the disciples. Simon Magus was baptized. Demas, who forsook Paul, had been counted a believer. Judas Iscariot was numbered with the apostles. The Redeemer does not want to lose one soul; His experience with Judas is recorded to show His long patience with perverse human nature; and He bids us bear with it as He has borne. *He has said that false brethren will be found in the church till the close of time.*
>
> Notwithstanding Christ's warning, men have sought to uproot the tares. To punish those who were supposed to be

1 *Christ's Object Lessons,* pp. 71-72 (emphasis added).

> evildoers, the church has had recourse to the civil power. Those who differed from the established doctrines have been imprisoned, put to torture and to death, at the instigation of men who claimed to be acting under the sanction of Christ. But it is the spirit of Satan, not the Spirit of Christ, that inspires such acts. This is Satan's own method of bringing the world under his dominion. God has been misrepresented through the church by this way of dealing with those supposed to be heretics. . . .
>
> The tares are permitted to grow among the wheat, to have all the advantage of sun and shower; but in the time of the harvest ye shall "return, and discern between the righteous and the wicked, between him that serveth God and him that serveth Him not." Mal. 3:18. *Christ Himself will decide who are worthy to dwell with the family of heaven. He will judge every man according to his words and his works.* Profession is as nothing in the scale. It is character that decides destiny.[2]

Jesus interpreted the details of His parable for the disciples:

> He that soweth the good seed is the Son of man; The field is the world; the good seed are the children of the kingdom; but the tares are the children of the wicked one; The enemy that sowed them is the devil; *the harvest is the end of the world; and the reapers are the angels.* As therefore the tares are gathered and burned in the fire; so shall it be in the end of this world. The Son of man shall send forth his angels, and they shall gather out of his kingdom all things that offend, and them which do iniquity; And shall cast them into a furnace of fire: there shall be wailing and gnashing of teeth (Matt 13:37-42).

Let us be clear in noting that it is the Lord, through His angels, who brings about a separation between the wheat and the tares, not the members or leaders of the church. We should not limit the Lord in how He will bring about this cleansing. The Spirit of Prophecy informs us about one process that separates the false from the true even now in probationary time. Note the following statement:

> The fact that there is no controversy or agitation among God's people, should not be regarded as conclusive evidence that they are holding fast to sound doctrine. There is reason to fear that they may not be clearly discriminating between truth

2 Ibid., pp. 72-74 (emphasis added).

> and error. When no new questions are started by investigation of the Scriptures, when no difference of opinion arises which will set men to searching the Bible for themselves, to make sure that they have the truth, there will be many now, as in ancient times, who will hold to tradition, and worship they know not what. . . .
>
> God will arouse His people; if other means fail, heresies will come in among them, which will sift them, separating the chaff from the wheat. The Lord calls upon all who believe His word to awake out of sleep. Precious light has come, appropriate for this time. It is Bible truth, showing the perils that are right upon us. This light should lead us to a diligent study of the Scriptures, and a most critical examination of the positions which we hold. . . .
>
> Agitate, agitate, agitate! The subjects which we present to the world must be to us a living reality. It is important that in defending the doctrines which we consider fundamental articles of faith, we should never allow ourselves to employ arguments that are not wholly sound. These may avail to silence an opposer, but they do not honor the truth. We should present sound arguments, that will not only silence our opponents, but will bear the closest and most searching scrutiny.[3]

According to these insights the Lord will overrule the presentation of false doctrines to purify His people. Those who hold to tradition will likewise be found wanting. How sad it is that the leaders and members of the Reform Movement refuse to search further lest they find something in their teaching that is not in full harmony with the Bible and Spirit of Prophecy. They consider themselves safe in holding to the teachings of their pioneers without change. This allows heresies to remain in the church. They are so intent on pointing out the faults of the Adventist Church that they cannot see their own.

Without doubt there are many tares within the Adventist Church as there are in the Reform Movement. There are members who are not truly converted. We may grieve about this matter, but it is not left with us to do the work of uprooting the tares. They will continue to be found in the church until the Lord works to remove them. The obligation facing us is to examine and to change our own lives lest we suffer the ultimate fate of the "tares."

3 Ellen G. White, *Gospel Workers* (Washington, DC: Review & Herald Publishing Assn., 1948), pp. 298-99.

Chapter 9

Conclusion

The friend who invites you to separate from the Seventh-day Adventist Church and become a member of the Reform Movement may be a fine Christian and have good intentions. He may assure you that in joining the Reform Movement you will be upholding the original teachings of the Advent Movement. No matter how sincere he may seem, or how honestly he may be deceived, nevertheless he is still deceived. He is promoting a bill of goods which simply does not deliver.

Even though the Reform Movement started as a seemingly logical protest against the wrong actions of the Adventist leadership in Europe, it is based on many false assumptions. One major assumption is that God has given up His long-suffering character and has become short-tempered because of the shortness of time. As a result, He has now rejected the Adventist movement He called forth because of one error made by a few men in Europe at the beginning of World War I!

This concept makes God a liar. He says, "I am the Lord, I change not" (Mal 3:6). He bore patiently with the repeated apostasies of ancient Israel and did not reject them as His chosen people until three and one-half years after they put His only Son to death.

We marvel at His long-suffering toward His chosen people. At the same time we can be so thankful for this wonderful attribute toward our wayward condition. The Lord was still with His people at the time of the death of His special messenger to the remnant in 1915. Through these same writings of the gift, God indicates He will be with the Advent people until the end of time.

While Reformers attempt to use the *Testimonies* in such a way as to indicate that Ellen White "prophesied" of another organization to come, the writings from her pen state just the opposite.

> The Lord has declared that the history of the past shall be rehearsed as we enter upon the closing work. Every truth that He has given for these last days is to be proclaimed to the world. Every pillar that He has established is to be strengthened. We cannot now step off the foundation that God established. *We*

> *cannot now enter into any new organization; for this would mean apostasy from the truth [1905].*[1]

> I am encouraged and blessed as I realize that the God of Israel is still guiding His people, and that He will continue to be with them, even to the end [1913].[2]

Although Reformers make a very high profession and claim to be the special chosen people of God, His remnant, this profession is not related to reality. The entire movement is filled with self-righteous egotism, the majority being brainwashed into believing that they are the only faithful followers of Jesus. There is no direct sin involved in being deceived, but attitudes become sinful when we close our minds to further instruction.

Describing the rejection in the final judgment of those who are told by the Lord, "I never knew you," the servant of the Lord writes:

> Here is the greatest deception that can affect the human mind; these persons believe that they are right when they are wrong. They think that they are doing a great work in their religious life, but Jesus finally tears off their self-righteous covering and vividly presents before them the true picture of themselves in all their wrongs and deformity of religious character. They are found wanting when it is forever too late to have their wants supplied. God has provided means to correct the erring: yet if those who err, choose to follow their own judgment, and despise the means which He has ordained to correct them and unite them upon the truth, they will be brought to the position described by the words of our Lord quoted above.[3]

> God will not condemn any at the judgment because they honestly believed a lie, or conscientiously cherished error; but it will be because they neglected the opportunities of making themselves acquainted with truth. The infidel will be condemned, not because he was an infidel, but because he did not take advantage of the means God has placed within his reach to enable him to become a Christian.[4]

I appeal to every member of the Reform Movement who may read this booklet. Open your eyes to the realities of the movement you are

---

1 *Selected Messages,* book. 2, p. 390 (emphasis added).
2 Ibid., p. 406.
3 *Testimonies for the Church,* 1:417.
4 *Testimonies to Ministers,* p. 437.

supporting. Look at its divided state and the many workers who have found it necessary to resign in order to live with their consciences. Open your Bibles and study the example left for us by our loving Lord. See the beauty of His matchless character. Listen to His words of pitying love as He spoke to the woman taken in adultery, "Neither do I condemn thee: go, and sin no more." Your leaders would have condemned Jesus just as the Jewish leaders did when He was upon earth. As you view the Saviour's matchless love for sinners, compare His compassion with the actions taken in the movement of which you are a member.

Secondly, begin to study the Spirit of Prophecy with an open mind to understand what the Lord is telling His people through His servant. Look up every statement which you have used to prove your position as a separate movement and read it in context. You may be surprised at what will be revealed to you by the Lord. As you study with an open mind, asking the Lord to guide you, new vistas will open before you. New insights into the love of Jesus will brighten your clouded mind. I believe the Lord will reveal your duty to you just as He did to me.

Open your heart and let the Saviour come in as never before. He is waiting to enter and give you the true peace and assurance of your salvation. You will have a new song in your heart. You who are still satisfied in your pharisaical pride, saying, "Lord, I thank thee that I am not like these Adventists," think about what happened to those self-satisfied people of old. Instead of following in their footsteps, open your heart's door to Jesus.

The Saviour says, "Behold, I stand at the door, and knock: if any man hear my voice, and open the door, I will come in to him, and will sup with him, and he with me" (Rev 3:20). This call is for each of us. Instead of fighting against that church which the Lord established to carry the last message to the ends of the earth, put your energies to good use in helping finish that work so we can all go home.

> Do you ask, What shall I do to be saved? You must lay your preconceived opinions, your hereditary and cultivated ideas, at the door of investigation. If you search the Scriptures to vindicate your own opinions, you will never reach the truth. Search in order to learn what the Lord says. If conviction comes as you search, if you see that your cherished opinions are not in harmony with the truth, do not misinterpret the truth in order to suit your own belief, but accept the light given. Open mind and heart that you may behold wondrous things out of God's word.[5]

5 *Christ's Object Lessons,* p. 112.

Only as you remove the blindfold which has been placed over your eyes by often well-meaning, but nonetheless deceived, leaders and fellow members will you be able to see the light of Christ's love. Do not believe all the stories you have been told about your brothers and sisters in the Adventist Church. While, without question, some who claim to be Adventists are not living the truth as you feel they should, it is also true that we are all sinners saved by the grace of Jesus Christ. He came to this world in order to save sinners. Allow love to replace condemnation. Be united with your faithful brethren who are taking the message of Christ to the ends of the earth rather than giving your monies to promote discord between yourselves and your brethren.

The family of God is waiting for you with love and understanding. Why not come back? I close with the appeal made by none other than Jesus Himself. "The Spirit and the bride say, 'Come!' And let him who hears say, 'Come!' Whoever is thirsty, let him come; and whoever wishes, let him take the free gift of the water of life" (Rev 22:17, NIV).